16527

THE OUTWARD BOUND STAYING WARM IN THE OUTDOORS HANDBOOK

THE OUTWARD BOUND STAYING WARM IN THE OUTDOORS HANDBOOK

Glenn Randall

The Lyons Press

CONTENTS

INTRODUCTION

The storm broke at sunset. Under clearing skies, the temperature dropped quickly to near zero, while the wind continued to blow plumes of fresh snow off the higher peaks. It was mid-March, and I was camped at 11,300 feet in the mountains south of Aspen, Colorado. I had come there to photograph the full moon setting over the rugged peaks of the Maroon Bells–Snowmass Wilderness at sunrise. Tomorrow morning—my forty-third birthday—would be my only chance, because another storm was forecast to arrive tomorrow afternoon. I could hardly sleep that night as I tried to envision the best possible way to capture the beauty I hoped to find. The combination of serious cold and wind made me wonder, however, whether I would be able to tolerate standing nearly immobile for over an hour while I set up and used my bulky, cumbersome 4×5 field camera.

My alarm jolted me awake at 2:45 A.M. the next morning. Moonlight reflecting off the new-fallen snow made my headlamp unnecessary as I snowshoed toward my shooting location atop a nearby 12,000-foot knoll. With each step, I monitored my body's temperature. It was imperative to neither sweat nor become chilled. Ten minutes below the summit, I paused to put on an extra sweater. I knew I would cool off when I took off my wind shell to add the sweater, then warm up again as I finished snowshoeing to the top.

I arrived on the summit an hour before sunrise—enough time

to finish donning the rest of my clothing and to find the best possible composition of the breathtaking scene before me. My investment in top-quality clothing and careful management of body temperature paid off: Twenty minutes before sunrise, comfortably warm, I made the most satisfying image of the entire trip: a shot of the moon hanging low in the cobalt blue sky over Cathedral Peak. Even more important than the image on film was the experience, indelibly imprinted in my memory, of being alone in winter in one of the most spectacular mountain ranges in the United States.

Enjoying winter's otherworldly beauty is just one of the many rewards of learning to deal with the cold. Adventure is another. Venturing deep into the winter wilderness presents challenges and offers satisfactions impossible to find amidst the crowds of summer. Lastly there's the simple, childlike joy of playing in the snow, whether on skis, snowshoes, or a snowboard.

In this book I've tried to distill the wisdom I've gleaned from close to thirty years of experience ice-climbing, skiing, snowshoeing, mountaineering, and camping in winter. My first experience on skis (sliding down a snow-filled drainage ditch alongside a road in West Virginia) whetted my appetite for more winter adventures and helped prompt my move to Colorado. With Colorado as my base, I launched expeditions to mountains from Alaska to Argentina. All told I've spent seven months on expeditions to some of the world's coldest mountains, including four expeditions to Mt. McKinley, the highest mountain in North America. What I've learned in the mountains about gear, my body, and how they interact has made it possible for me to enjoy being outside in almost any kind of frigid weather. Those experiences also taught me another crucial lesson: Staying warm in the cold has nothing whatsoever to do with being tough. With the knowledge in this book, the right gear, and a little bit of your own experience, you, too, can truly enjoy the most demanding and rewarding season of all: winter.

1

SECOND SKINS: LONG UNDERWEAR AND THE PHYSIOLOGY OF SWEAT

The most rapid drop in body temperature I've ever experienced was not on Mt. McKinley, where the climate only halfway to the summit is equivalent to the North Pole's. Instead, it was in Arizona, on a hot, sunny afternoon. How did I get so chilled?

I was traversing Clear Creek Canyon, a narrow high-desert gorge with tall sandstone walls that, in places, drop directly into the creek. The only way through the narrowest portions of the gorge is to lash your pack to an inner tube and swim. When I emerged from each swim the rapid evaporation of water from my skin in the bone-dry air set my teeth to chattering instantly.

It was an unforgettable lesson in the power of evaporation to steal heat from my body—a lesson that's even more applicable to winter adventures than it is to summer hikes. The first and most important lesson beginners must learn about winter is that staying warm means staying dry.

"What is warm when wet? A hot tub!" wrote Jack Stephenson in his Warmlite Equipment catalog. Nothing else truly is. To stay warm in the cold, you must know the insidious ways of water. Water is everywhere—in snow, rain, air, your breath, your sweat.

The physics of water dictate the terms of cold-weather comfort in more ways, literally, than meet the eye.

WHY SWEATING MAKES YOU COLD

Let's start with sweat. Sweat, obviously, is intended to cool you—and it does this with a vengeance. It takes an enormous amount of heat energy to make sweat evaporate. This heat energy is sucked directly out of your body. That's a blessing if you're slogging across the Sahara under the midday sun, but a potential disaster in the cold once you stop the heat-producing activity that generated the sweat.

Your body can produce sweat at rates ranging from nearly zero to quarts per hour. Let's say you sweat out just half a quart between breakfast and lunch, an easy thing to do if you're careless about heat regulation. Evaporation of that much sweat requires as much energy as is needed to raise the temperature of two gallons of water by 61 degrees. Think of setting a two-gallon bucket of ice-cold water on your stomach and warming it to a comfortable lukewarm temperature of 93 degrees with body heat alone. The amount of heat lost becomes apparent.

Well, if you're overheating, what's wrong with sweating, even if it's cold? Several things. First, that sweat is only about 50 percent effective in cooling you compared to its effectiveness in evaporating from bare skin in the summertime. The reason is that much of that sweat vapor never escapes your clothing. The amount of moisture that air can hold depends on its temperature. The warm air next to your skin can hold lots of moisture. But as that warm, moist air heads toward the cooler outer layers of your clothing, much of the moisture condenses. When water vapor condenses back into liquid water, it gives up the heat it absorbed when it evaporated. The net result is ineffective cooling and continued overheating, which leads to more sweat produced and more water trapped in your clothing.

Trapped sweat not only ruins the effectiveness of some insulations, but it also creates a tremendous "heat debt" that you have to pay back as soon as you stop moving. Let's say you finally arrive at camp after several hours of skiing steadily uphill. Almost immediately, your body's heat production will drop to about one-fifth of the level it reached when you were active. Any sweat trapped inside your clothing is still there, however. It will distribute itself through your clothing until it gets close enough to your skin for your body's warmth to force it to evaporate again. Your skin is also likely to be wet from sweat that hadn't evaporated at the time you quit moving. The amount of heat extracted by evaporation will be the same as when you were active, but your much-diminished heat output at rest will no longer be adequate to replace the lost heat. Soon you'll be shivering.

The first secret to staying warm, then, is staying cool—cool enough so that you sweat the minimum amount possible. That means stopping to adjust your clothing as soon as you start to overheat. Too many people overdress in the wintertime. They're afraid of getting cold, and so they bundle up like a thin man in a Halloween fat costume. The most extreme example of this that I've heard of occurred in 1965. A soldier was admitted to the hospital in Fort Wainwright, Alaska, who had been chopping wood outside when it was 40 below. The diagnosis: heatstroke. The cause: too much clothing.

WHY SOME SWEAT IS INEVITABLE

Avoiding sweating in the winter sounds simple, doesn't it? After all, it's *cold* out there. Unfortunately, your body's physiology dictates otherwise.

You may think you actively sweat only when your skin feels hot. You're only half right. True, when skin temperature rises above normal, a spinal reflex tells the sweat glands in your skin to get cranking. But you also start sweating when your core temperature goes up through physical activity. Heat production during maximum exertion can reach twenty times the amount produced when you're sitting still. That increase can only be sustained for a few minutes, but a five-fold increase can be sustained for hours. In either case, your hot muscles heat your blood. The temperature regulator in your hypothalamus, a section of your brain, then stimulates the sweat glands to get rid of that excess heat. Even if some areas of your skin are cold, other areas may perspire. Your back is often one such area because your pack, usually filled with extra clothing and a sleeping bag, adds a lot of insulation to that part of your body.

Another common sweat source is your head. For most of your body, the brain controls the diameter of blood vessels near the skin, opening them wide when there is heat to be disposed of, closing them down when the body's core needs every warm drop of blood it can get. The opening of the blood vessels is called vasodilatation. The closing down is called vasoconstriction. Blood vessels near the skin in most of your body also respond to skin temperature, closing down when the skin is cold, opening up when it's warm. Blood flow at maximum is one hundred times greater than at minimum.

These mechanisms don't affect your head, however. That's why working hard in the cold sometimes causes the sweat of your brow to run into your eyes at the same time your hands feel like numb claws. Your core is warm, and that warm blood is circulating vigorously through your head, causing the skin to sweat. However, the blood vessels in your hands, if exposed to cold enough air, can be constricting while your head is sweating, so your hands feel cold. This phenomenon is why you sometimes see marathon runners wearing shorts, a T-shirt, and gloves. It's also why your head and neck can provide the escape hatch for as much as 25 to 50 percent of your total heat loss.

The old saying, "If your feet are cold, put on a hat," is based on these facts as well. Your feet are a long way from your core, which means blood is already cooling when it gets there. Your feet also have a larger surface area in relation to their volume than your torso. That means a proportionally greater area from which to lose heat. And your feet are well supplied with sweat glands, with about 4,000 per square inch compared to 640 per square inch on your back. Evaporative heat loss can be high. If you start to get a little chilly, your brain restricts blood flow to your feet and they start to get cold. Putting on a hat helps stem that overall heat loss. Your body now has some warm blood to spare, so it responds by sending some out to your nippy toes. Usually that's enough to warm them up, at least eventually. Your hands get cold easily for the same reasons that your toes do. Wearing a hat can help keep them warm, too.

Avoiding sweating entirely, even in a cold environment, is also difficult because, in some primeval way, we like it. Researchers at Kansas State University's Institute for Environmental Research found that people exercising in a test chamber considered themselves more comfortable when they were sweating than when they weren't. The harder they worked, the more sweat they were producing when they declared themselves most comfortable, even though they had the option of cooling the test chamber until they stopped sweating completely.

How do you deal with the small amount of sweat even the most savvy wilderness traveler produces? By wearing clothing next to your skin that keeps you as comfortable as possible, even when damp. As we shall see, different clothing fibers differ dramatically in their ability to keep you comfortable in winter weather.

COTTON: THE WORST COLD-WEATHER MATERIAL

I've learned the hard way (several times, I have to confess) that cotton is absolutely the wrong material for cold-weather use. The most recent occasion when I got that lesson frozen into my skin was during an hour-long spring training ride on my bicycle. The sun, which had been beating down when I started, had tempted me to leave the house wearing nothing on my back but a cotton T-shirt. I had noticed the black cloud looming up over the foothill peaks just west of my home in Boulder, Colorado, but with cocky nonchalance, I thought I would be home before the storm hit.

I wasn't. I was still eight miles from safety when a ferocious rainstorm broke loose, accompanied by gale-force winds. I was soon forced to stand up in my lowest gear to make progress on level ground, and even then I could only struggle forward at a walking pace. The pelting rain immediately plastered the T-shirt to my skin. I became so miserable that when a passing driver asked if I wanted a lift, I gratefully accepted.

Cotton sucks up water like a thirsty camel in the desert. In textile jargon, its "moisture regain" is about 15 percent, making it one of the most absorbent of all fibers. That means that a completely dry sample placed in a chamber at 70 degrees with 95 percent relative humidity will absorb 15 percent of its weight in water. Moisture regain is the textile industry's standard method of assessing a fabric's affinity for water. They use this method, rather than measuring how much water a fabric soaks up when immersed, because fabrics hold liquid water in two ways—by actual absorption into the fiber and by surface tension. Surface tension is the force that makes a drop of water sitting on a flat surface mound up into a hemispherical shape. Remember making bubbles as a kid by dipping the bubble wand's circular opening into soapy water, then blowing through the loop? Surface tension is the force that holds the soap film in a spherical shape.

All fabrics hold water by surface tension. Cotton, however, also actually absorbs water. The absorbed water then acts to soften the long cellulose molecules that make up cotton. The result: The cotton molecule loses all its resiliency. A dry cotton fiber is six times stiffer than a wet one. Wet cotton fabrics collapse and cling to your skin. Low-life brew pubs take advantage of this fact when they conduct wet T-shirt contests. The clinging fabric forces all the water the fabric is holding to evaporate directly off your skin, extracting the maximum possible amount of heat from your shivering body.

In addition, wet cotton conducts heat much faster than dry cotton. A completely saturated cotton T-shirt conducts heat about ten times as fast as a dry one. Cotton also dries very slowly. Cotton has no place in my outdoor wardrobe in either winter or summer, and it shouldn't in yours.

WOOL: PUT THIS OLD STAND-BY OUT TO PASTURE

Wool is even more absorbent than cotton, with about a 29 percent moisture regain. Some textile textbooks call that an advantage because you feel dryer longer. However, a typical wool underwear top only weighs eight or nine ounces. You can sweat enough to saturate the garment in an hour or two if you ignore an overheating problem.

Another supposed advantage of wool is that the condensation of water vapor as it is absorbed into a dry sweater actually releases heat. That could happen when a sweater is taken from a warm, dry house into the outdoors on a chilly day, for example. However, this reaction only occurs when water *vapor* (not liquid water like sweat or rain) is absorbed into the fiber. It still costs heat energy to drive that water back out again.

Wool does resist collapse when wetted, so it still provides some insulation. Generations of backwoods moms and dads have raised their kids to wear wool in the wintertime. It still works. But, like cotton, wool dries very slowly. I got a graphic demonstration of that in 1978, during my first expedition to Alaska. After a week of rain and wet snow, every garment we owned was soaked. When the sun finally came out, we festooned every ski, ice axe, and ski pole with sodden garments. Among them was a knitted synthetic sweater, fuzzy inside, smooth outside. It was one of the first nylon fleece garments I'd ever seen. Within an hour the fleece sweater was warm and dry. At sundown the wool sweater was still damp. I put on the fleece and jammed the wool sweater into a stuff sack, where it remained, useless, for the rest of the thirty-five-day trip. Wool also makes many people itch like they've got the chicken pox (I get a rash if I wear it when I'm sweating) and it's considerably less abrasion-resistant than the synthetics.

SILK: ANOTHER ALSO-RAN

A few companies offer winter underwear made of silk. Although it feels wonderful next to the skin, silk has a moisture regain comparable to wool. It dries slowly, is fragile compared to the synthetics, usually requires extra care when washing, and is quite expensive. The best synthetics are a much better alternative.

SYNTHETICS: THE FIBER OF CHOICE

The best winter underwear today is knitted from fibers made of polyester, nylon, or polypropylene. None of these fibers absorb water. All retain their full resiliency when wet, so all work much better than any of the natural fibers when used in long underwear. The differences among the synthetics are in the details.

Polypropylene was the first synthetic to become popular as winter underwear. Back in the early 1960s, some oil refineries were burning propylene (the building block for polypropylene), because they couldn't find enough companies willing to buy it. Lifa, headquartered in Norway, was probably the first company to make polypro underwear. Their stuff was nothing romantic. It didn't go to Everest for its trial run. Instead, it was first used in babies' diapers.

The first polypro underwear to arrive in the United States was very thin. A myth began to spread that "polypropylene wasn't warm in itself" and that it had to be used beneath other underwear. In truth, like all synthetics, polypropylene's warmth is proportional to its thickness, as people realized when thicker versions became available.

Polypropylene does have drawbacks. One is its low melting point, which means it must be washed in cold water and line-dried to avoid shrinkage. Wash it hot and you'll have doll clothes. Another drawback is its tendency to amplify body odors.

The fiber of choice these days for long underwear seems to be polyester. Polyester has a moisture regain of less than one percent and doesn't lose its resiliency when wet, so it meets the two fundamental criteria for winter underwear. Some of the new versions have a better "hand" (textile lingo for feeling good on your skin) than polypropylene, which can develop a rather plastic feel. Polyester is inherently more stable when heated than polypro, which means you can throw it in the washer and dryer. Polyester underwear also doesn't magnify body odors like polypro does.

Polyester can be treated so it wicks. Water will then flow along the fiber from wet areas to dry ones. Water creeping up a small-diameter glass tube is an example of the same principle. Wicking's advantage is that it subtracts moisture from your skin without subtracting heat the way evaporation does. The moisture passes out into the outer layers of your clothing, where, at least in some conditions, some of the heat for evaporating it can come from the environment. Wicking also makes the fabric next to your skin dry faster by spreading the moisture over a larger area where more air can get to it. Visualize how long it takes for a glass of water to evaporate. Now picture how long it would take if you spread the same amount of water out on a sidewalk.

Nylon is also used in a few brands of long underwear. Nylon is the strongest and most abrasion-resistant of the synthetic fibers commonly used in underwear, but it doesn't have quite as soft a hand as the best polyester underwear. Like polypropylene and polyester, it retains its resiliency when wet.

No one has yet found a way to freeze-dry a hot tub. Until someone does, you'll only be comfortable if you stay dry by avoiding perspiring and by wearing synthetic underwear. Stay dry, and you'll find that staying warm is no sweat.

2

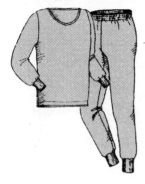

FLORIDA IN THE ARCTIC: THE SURPRISE OF VAPOR-BARRIER CLOTHING

Ounce for ounce, the warmest clothing you can buy is also the least understood. I'm talking about vapor-barrier shirts, pants, socks, and sleeping bag liners.

Vapor-barrier garments are made of lightweight, waterproof fabric. They're designed to be worn as an inner layer, generally next to your skin or one layer away. They work by stopping evaporative heat loss. A complete suit of vapor-barrier clothes can block fully 15 percent of your normal heat loss, yet shirt, pants, and socks together weigh only half a pound, about the same as one medium-weight polyester turtleneck.

VB clothes have an additional virtue: They warn you the moment you start to overheat. You can then stop and shed a layer before sweat can soak your clothes. If you do sweat a little even after shedding, wearing VB clothing lets you stop moving without instantly developing the shivers.

"But don't you sweat to death?" most people ask. Not necessarily. As the first chapter explained, you actively sweat only when a portion of your skin overheats, or when your core overheats, or both. You can keep active sweating to a minimum by carefully regulating the amount of insulation you're wearing. My friends and I routinely stop to strip down fifteen minutes after we start up from any extended rest. We make other clothing-adjustment stops as necessary. Don't worry about holding up the rest of the team. You'll slow them down much more (besides endangering yourself) if evaporation from your sweat-saturated clothing chills you severely when you finally do stop.

Whether you wear a vapor barrier or not, sweating will extract its price. Without a vapor barrier, you pay it by being unpleasantly hot when you're moving, by losing excessive amounts of fluid, and by developing the shivers when you stop as the sweat evaporates from your saturated clothing. With a vapor barrier, sweating without any evaporative cooling soon becomes so uncomfortable that you stop and shed clothing, as you should, rather than slogging on in your own version of Bogart wading chest-deep down the river in *The African Queen*.

THE VAPOR-BARRIER PRINCIPLE

Here's how vapor barriers work. Your body is about 57 percent water by weight. Much of that water lies between cells, not inside them. Because your skin is not like a plastic bag, some of that water is constantly evaporating—and when you're fighting to stay warm, that hurts. This water loss, called insensible perspiration because you don't sense its presence, goes on night and day, with no nervous system control, at the rate of about half a quart every twenty-four hours. Roughly 15 percent of the total heat lost by a sedentary person escapes through evaporation of insensible perspiration. VB shirts, pants, and socks stop almost all of that evaporative heat loss.

Using vapor-barrier clothing effectively does require some practice. Listen to Yvon Chouinard, world-traveling mountaineer and founder of Patagonia, describe his experiences.

"I experimented with vapor-barrier shirts in 1974 but dropped the idea because I didn't like it. I didn't understand the concept too well, and I found I couldn't regulate the warmth very much. I found that most of the time I was too sweaty. I had to keep taking things off. Where I really got sold on it was fly-fishing in late October in Yellowstone for brown trout. I was wearing chest waders, pile pants, long underwear, pile booties, lightweight polypropylene, heavy polypropylene, pile jacket, wool shirt, waterproof anorak, and a wool hat. I was standing all day long in 40-degree water up to my waist. The wind was blowing, it was snowing, the temperature was near freezing. I wasn't moving enough to stay warm and all my heat was being drawn away by this cold water. I could not stay warm, no matter how thick an insulation I used. Finally I used a vapor-barrier shirt as well. I found I could cut down on the insulation and still stay warm. I've used it on every expedition since."

Doing something outdoors in the cold that demands little exertion is the best place to start experimenting with VB clothing. Wearing VB clothing while ice-fishing, sitting in a duck blind, or just cooking a meal demonstrates the strength of the concept. Few people overdress so extravagantly that they actively sweat when standing still. Everyone loses insensible perspiration even when they're inactive, however. VB clothing stops that heat loss. It also keeps your outer insulation dry and prevents condensation on the inside of waterproof rain gear, further adding to your warmth.

Used correctly, VB clothing can also be valuable in more strenuous sports. First, be sure to shed clothing when you first start to overheat. Unzip the VB shirt at the neck, open the cuffs, and unzip the VB pants at the sides if they're equipped with such zippers. If you're not wearing a pack, pull the shirt tails out of your pants. This will help promote ventilation through the "chimney effect": Cool air enters at the bottom, is warmed by your body, and rises inside the shirt, absorbing moisture as it goes, before escaping at the neck. The shirt "draws" just like a chimney. When you stop, batten down the hatches to halt the instant chill-down so common when you quit moving in the winter.

Since it's very difficult to avoid at least a little sweating when working hard, you'll probably trap a little moisture inside the VB garments. Don't worry about it. Leave the VB garments closed up when you're resting or puttering around camp. Later, when you move on and start putting out lots of heat again, or when you snuggle into your bag and have lots more insulation, you can open up the VB clothing and finish drying out.

Many people find that wearing a VB garment next to their skin feels rather odd. I recommend wearing a thin, nonabsorbent layer of underwear between your skin and the vapor barrier. That system lengthens the time between the onset of sweating and when you first notice the sweat, meaning more sweat gets produced, but seems to be more comfortable. This approach has the added advantage of reducing friction between your clothing layers, providing freer movement. Try it both ways and see what you like best.

Vapor-barrier clothing presents more advantages and fewer

drawbacks as the temperature plummets. When I first bought a VB shirt I put it on next to my skin, added one thin layer on top and went for a bike ride on a windy, 40-degree day. To my astonishment, I was simply too hot. For active sports, I'd recommend VB clothing only for temperatures below freezing. It really comes into its own on days when unprotected water bottles freeze solid before noon— days when the high might be zero and the low 20 or 30 below. For inactive sports, some people recommend its use in temperatures below 65. Personally, I do quite well with conventional clothing down into the 20s, even when I'm inactive.

VAPOR-BARRIER SOCKS

My first experiment with VB socks surprised me as much as that ride with the VB shirt. I put a plastic bag over a liner sock, then added a heavy wool sock and put the whole thing into a double mountaineering boot with a foam inner bootie and stiff outer plastic shell. On the other foot I wore the same layers without the plastic bag. Then I went for a hike in November in Rocky Mountain National Park. It proved to be fairly warm for late fall, with temperatures in the 40s. Two miles into the hike, I had to stop and remove the plastic bag. That foot was almost painfully hot.

VB socks have proved their worth many times over on colder days. I wore the same boots and socks, plus the vapor-barrier socks, when it was 40 below at 17,000 feet on McKinley. My toes grew cold, but didn't freeze.

When wearing VB socks, be sure to give your feet a chance to air out. My nightly procedure on McKinley was to remove the damp liner socks and pour a little athlete's foot powder onto my toes. The powder not only felt great, it helped dry the skin and prevented my toes from sprouting mushrooms. The foot powder's strong perfume also prevented my tent mates (and me!) from gagging on the odor of feet unwashed for a month straight. Then I put on spare liner socks that I had dried the previous night inside my clothing while I was asleep. The wet socks I had just removed went down inside my bibs to be dried in their turn. During the night the VB socks remained outside the sleeping bag. In the morning I turned them inside out, brushed off any frost, and put them on. Leaving your VB socks on for several days straight turns your feet into prunes, which makes them quite susceptible to blistering and a serious cold injury called trenchfoot, which I'll discuss fully later. People with hyperhidrosis (excessive sweating of the hands and feet) are particularly susceptible to these problems. About ten percent of the population has this condition. These people may find that their feet get so wet so quickly that VB socks do more harm than good.

VAPOR-BARRIER SLEEPING-BAG LINERS

Sleep is another sedentary activity where the VB principle works superbly. Using a VB sleeping-bag liner lets most people sleep comfortably in temperatures ten to 15 degrees colder than they could tolerate in their sleeping bag alone. Using a VB liner is particularly important when using a down bag because down loses loft when it gets wet. I usually leave my VB liner open at the neck. That allows some moisture to escape from my clothes while I'm asleep without that moisture condensing inside my down bag. If I'm fighting for every bit of warmth I can get, then I cinch the VB liner down tightly. Although a VB liner helps tremendously to keep your bag warm and lofty, it's still important on long trips to take advantage of every opportunity to dry your sleeping bag.

3

THE WELL-DRESSED ONION: LAYERING FOR VERSATILE WARMTH

My sister Amy calls it her "goose": a plump, warm, goose-down jacket. She took it and one thin sweater when we went skiing on a blustery February day near Berthoud Pass, Colorado. In total, she easily had enough insulation; but the disadvantage of its form soon became apparent. Fifteen minutes into the tour, she started cooking inside her goose and had to stow it. Without it, however, the wind soon gave her a chill. On went the goose again, quickly followed by another cycle of overheating.

Amy's "goose" is a great garment for winter bird-watching, but not so good for a one-day ski trip. No one would willingly start a hilly bike ride on a machine with only one or two gears. Similarly, no one should go into the winter wilderness with just one or two garments, no matter how heavy.

The layers of clothes you bring in the winter should be like the corn-cob cluster of tightly spaced gears bike racers use. They want a very close match between their maximum sustained output of energy and the particular gear best suited to the terrain. To achieve this, each gear differs only a little from the adjacent one. In a similar fashion, you should bring many thin layers of clothing when you venture into the cold. That way you can accurately fine-tune the amount of insulation you're wearing to correspond to your heat output and the vagaries of temperature, altitude, and wind.

THE CLOTHING SYSTEM

When you're wearing a lot of layers, it's important to think in terms of a system. Pile up all the clothing you need for the severe cold of the Alaska Range or Yellowstone in winter, for example, and it looks like it will fill a small trash can. Your outer layers have to fit over a tremendous amount of bulk, which often means going up a full size, particularly in parkas and shell gear. Some high-end manufacturers design their clothing to work as a system without the need to select the next larger size for outer layers. In other words, a medium parka, in their system, is designed to fit over several other medium garments. The only way to make sure everything works together is to try on every garment simultaneously before the trip.

If it's a major expedition you're planning, you need to get your gear together months in advance so you can test it on several overnight trips. The little annoyances you'll find during such dry runs (or wet runs, if the gear's really faulty!) will become major hassles after a week of continuous cold. One of the most important lessons I've learned from sustained cold-weather expeditions is that the details make a big difference in comfort.

Every zipper, for example, whether on your clothing, your pack, your tent, or your sleeping bag, should have a loop of string tied through the pull tab on the slider so you can grab it with gloves on. Do your pants tend to work their way down when carrying a heavy pack? Think about buying suspenders. Then try them out, too. It may be that the buckles will end up underneath the pack waist belt or shoulder straps and chafe.

Do you have enough pockets inside your clothes? You'll find you want to keep many little things handy or warm: sun block for your skin, a different sun block for your lips, a cigarette lighter or two (for the stove, not for cigarettes!), a pocket knife, and perhaps film and an extra battery for your camera. Look for both shell clothing and insulating clothing that offers lots of pockets.

How much trouble is it to get into those pockets? Pockets closed with hook-and-loop (the most common trade name is Velcro) are a pain in the fingers in the winter. The hook part scratches your fingers if they're bare or latches onto your gloves if they're not. I prefer pockets closed with zippers.

Snaps provide another source of frustration for numb, begloved fingers. I've seen snaps on gaiters freeze so hard that it took ten minutes of prying with a Swiss Army knife's screwdriver blade while simultaneously thawing with a lighter to get them open.

As part of your gear prep, carefully check every item of used equipment. Think about how many times a year you actually use your winter paraphernalia. Let's say you're pretty enthusiastic and average one day a week for five months. That's about twenty days of use in a whole year. You can give your old clothing that much use, the equivalent of a full year, in just three weeks during a big trip. Inspect each item you plan to bring and ask yourself if it can really endure another year of normal use. Check each seam of each garment by turning it inside out and trying gently to pull the seam apart. Are there places where the thread has worn through or some careless seamstress didn't backstitch a hem? Fix them.

If you can't fix your old gear, or you don't think the fabric itself has enough life left, buy new—then go test it. There's nothing more frustrating than landing on the glacier with brand-new equipment and finding that the gear had some hidden defect that causes it to fail at the first test. On my second trip to Alaska, our pilot dropped us off, without a radio, beneath the 6,000-foot south face of Mt. Hunter. One of my companions cinched down the spindrift collar on his shiny new pack and promptly ripped the drawstring completely out of its sleeve. My other companion discovered that the waist belt buckle on his new pack could simply slide off, which it had apparently done somewhere in transit. He carried the entire weight of his pack on his shoulders for the rest of the trip.

A bit wiser after that experience, I turned two new pair of gloves and a new pair of overmitts inside out before embarking on a big trip a few years later. All four of the gloves had a place where the lining had not been stitched down properly. The seam at the end of one overmitt liner had a gap where the sewing machine had simply missed the fabric. Checking these kinds of details in the store, before you buy, will save you from fixing them frantically at midnight the night before your trip.

As you're assembling and testing your clothing system, think about ventilation. If it's easy to vent excess heat without stopping, you're more likely to do it than if you have to stop, doff your pack, strip, load the pack, put it back on, and readjust the pack harness. Easy ventilation means zippers in strategic locations, like down your chest, under your arms, and down the sides of your legs. If you're wearing pants (rather than bibs), try to get them with double-pull zippers so you can unzip from the ankle up to put them on, then unzip them from the waist down to ventilate them. Better yet, get separating double-pull zippers so you can unzip from the ankle up, then separate the zipper halves at the waist. That allows you to get your pants on or off even while wearing skis, snowshoes, or crampons. Conventional knitted or woven pants rarely feature this kind of zipper, but they're common on good fleece pants.

Pants work fine in moderate cold, but when the temperature plummets, they take second place to bibs for several reasons. First, cold air can rush into that annoying gap that appears between your pants and jacket when you bend over. Second, the belt frequently required to keep pants up can chafe under a pack or sled-pulling harness. Third, that belt also prevents air from flowing from your hard-working and therefore warm legs to your cooler torso. Wearing a pair of bibs, or very high-waisted pants with suspenders, lets that warm air circulate throughout your clothing. Bibs also close the gap at your waist and prevent chafing by a belt.

If you choose bibs, make sure they have a "dumpster": some kind of crotch zipper or zippered drop seat to let you relieve yourself easily. Lack of a dumpster forces you to remove every layer outside your bibs whenever you have to go. In stormy weather that usually includes your shell jacket. Removing that lets snow and wind in, and a lot of heat out.

Climbers in extremely cold environments sometimes use one-piece, insulated suits. Warm air can circulate freely inside the suit, and no heat can escape at the waist, so one-piece suits are very comfortable when it's bitterly cold. One-piece suits lack versatility, however. Too often you find yourself wanting your shell jacket, but not your shell pants. Not many people really need such specialized clothing, so one-piece suits are expensive and hard to find.

HEAT LOSS AND INSULATION

No clothing (with the exception of electric socks) actually generates heat. All clothing can do is slow the loss of heat generated by your body. Besides evaporation, heat can be lost in three ways: conduction, convection, and radiation. If you understand these processes, you'll have a better understanding of how different kinds of insulators work. That helps you build a clothing system that suits your needs, and helps you avoid getting taken by some salesman's hype. So take a deep breath, hold on to your pocketbook, and let's dive in.

Brrr! It's cold in here! That's because the heat from your body is conducting into this cold water. Conduction is the process in which the energy of hot molecules is transmitted by collision to cooler, less energetic molecules. It can account for more than half of the total heat lost through clothing.

Conduction actually causes heat loss in two ways: through the clothing fibers themselves, and through the air the clothing traps. In knitted and woven fabrics, conduction through the clothing fibers can account for 50 to 80 percent of the total heat lost through conduction. That's because the fibers take up ten to 40 percent of the fabric's volume and because the heat conductivity of the fiber is about ten times the conductivity of air.

In high-loft insulators, on the other hand, such as down and the polyester fiberfills, the insulating fibers take up only about one percent of the volume. Those fibers don't run directly from one surface to the other like little pillars holding up a roof. Instead, most run at an angle to the shell fabrics, which slows conductive heat loss through the fiber still further. Even a steel wool batting, with highly conductive fibers, is only about 12 percent less insulating than a wool one of equivalent thickness, according to the Army's Research Institute of Environmental Medicine in Natick, Massachusetts.

Although the conductivity of air is much lower than the conductivity of polyester, conduction through air itself is significant because air takes up much more space inside the insulator. Air's conductivity is not worth worrying about, however, because there's nothing you can do about it short of wearing a steel vacuum bottle as a shirt.

Climb out of the pond now, towel off before the evaporation chills you, and grab a cup of hot tea. See the steam rising off the cup? That's an example of spontaneous convection. The warm, steamy air just above the cup is less dense than the cold air. Air heated by a warm object tends to float upward. Cool air then replaces the warm air, to be warmed and float upward in its turn. A convection current is born.

Spontaneous convection was once thought to be a major avenue of heat loss in clothing. More recent work at Canada's Defense Research Establishment and Natick, however, has shown that convection plays almost no role in heat transfer through battings with a fiber content as low as .2 percent by volume. A batting with that few fibers is practically transparent. Convection plays a significant role in heat transfer through air only when no fibers are interposed.

Convection doesn't have to be spontaneous; it can also be forced. Your movements, or high winds pummeling your clothing, can squeeze warm air out of gaps in your clothing at your waist, neck, wrists, and ankles. Cooler air is sucked back in, resulting in a net loss of heat. If you're not wearing a windproof shell garment, wind can also force its way in between the fibers of your clothing, displacing warm air and replacing it with cold air. If, in addition, you're wet, watch out! Wind also increases the rate of evaporation. A wet person without windproof clothing on a cold, windy day is in real trouble.

Equivalent Temperature (°F)

Calm	35	30	25	20	15	10	5	0	−5	−10	−15	−20	−25	−30	−35	−40	−45
5	32	27	22	16	11	6	0	−5	−10	−15	−21	−26	−31	−36	−42	−47	−52
10	22	16	10	3	−3	−9	−15	−22	−27	−34	−40	−46	−52	−58	−64	−71	−77
15	16	9	2	5	−11	−18	−25	−31	−38	−45	−51	−58	−65	−72	−78	−85	−92
20	12	4	−3	−10	−17	−24	−31	−39	−46	−53	−60	−67	−74	−81	−88	−95	−103
25	8	1	−7	−15	−22	−29	−36	−44	−51	−59	−66	−74	−81	−88	−96	−103	−110
30	6	−2	−10	−18	−25	−33	−41	−49	−56	−64	−71	−79	−86	−93	−101	−109	−116
35	4	−4	−12	−20	−27	−35	−43	−52	−58	−67	−74	−82	−89	−97	−105	−113	−120
40	3	−5	−13	−21	−29	−37	−45	−53	−60	−69	−76	−84	−92	−100	−107	−115	−123
45	2	−6	−14	−22	−30	−38	−46	−54	−62	−70	−78	−85	−93	−102	−109	−117	−125

(Zones labeled across the chart: COLD, VERY COLD, BITTER COLD, EXTREME COLD)

Wind Speed MPH

WIND CHILL CHART

Heat loss through forced convection is the origin of the "wind-chill factor": the apparent drop in temperature caused by wind. Paul Siple came up with the original wind-chill formula after studying the rate at which bottles of water froze in Antarctica under different conditions of wind and temperature. Conditions with equal freezing times were considered equivalent. Wind-chill temperatures apply primarily to the rate at which bare flesh freezes. The risk of frostbite on a windy day is much greater than on a day with the same temperature and no wind.

Still shivering after your dip in the pond? Perhaps you can build a fire. If you do, much of the heat you feel will travel to you in the form of infrared radiation. Hold something as thin as a sheet of paper in front of your face, and you'll notice an immediate drop in the heat you're receiving. That's because the paper is blocking most of the radiation.

Radiation and conduction together account for nearly all the heat passing through clothing. In a vacuum, radiation travels in a straight shot. In clothing, however, radiation travels a tortuous path, emitted, absorbed, and re-radiated over and over again as it bounces about among the fibers. The denser the insulation, the more times the radiation must be absorbed and re-radiated before escaping. Net heat loss is reduced. Using fibers of the right size also reduces heat loss through radiation. The right size turns out to be about ten microns. Some parts of a down plumule and some microfibers have that diameter (more about this later).

Another way to cut back the loss of radiant heat is through placing a reflector in the clothing system. Compared to a clothing fiber, shiny metallic surfaces not only reflect radiation, they also cut back on the radiant heat emitted. Radiant barriers are most effective when facing a dead air space. Practically speaking, that means they must be either the outermost layer in a clothing system (and face outward) or be integrated into a very low density layer of insulation, such as a down or fiberfill jacket.

Furthermore, they must indeed be reflective, in other words, shiny. While the "wet look" may once have been fashionable at downhill ski areas, few people want to look like a walking advertisement for Reynolds Wrap. Any coating or fabric laminate to reduce the space-oddity appearance or increase the durability of the reflective layer also decreases the value of the radiant barrier. Compression by quilting the batting or squashing it beneath a pack also reduces the efficiency, as does contact with any conductive material. A wood stove provides a good analogy. When made of blackened iron, the stove's radiation can be felt halfway across the room. If made of shiny stainless steel, however, you would hardly know the stove was hot—until you touched it. Conduction would then immediately drain the stove's heat into your hand. Coatings act like your hand, draining heat away.

Conventional fabrics, such as those used in long johns and the various fleeces, are dense enough to deal with the radiation component of heat loss pretty effectively through absorption and re-radiation. Adding a reflective layer gives little additional warmth. Beware of advertising hype giving insulation values for some reflective barrier used alone. Adding the reflective barrier to a glove or fleece jacket won't necessarily add the full insulation value of the reflective (measured alone) to the garment. The increase in insulation value will probably be much lower.

Reflectives do have some practical value in very low density bats of insulation, such as found in parkas and sleeping bags. Data from Du Pont shows that adding four reflective barriers to a Hollofil 808 polyester batting adds about 40 percent to the insulation value. If, instead of adding reflectives, you add a weight of batting equivalent to the weight of the reflectives, you only get 20 percent more insulation. Down on its own handles radiation better than the low-density synthetics so you won't see as much benefit from reflectives.

CHOOSING YOUR MIDDLEWEIGHT LAYERS

Understanding modes of heat loss is most important in choosing a parka. Beneath your parka and above your long underwear, however, you need one or several middleweight layers. For these layers, look for garments made of material that won't absorb water so they'll dry fast and retain their loft when damp. Wool's just too moisture-loving for my taste. So what does that leave you? Mostly garments made from that synthetic, furry-looking material that was once called pile and is now usually referred to as fleece.

Fleece fabrics are made using many techniques. Some give a fabric that has a furry appearance on one side, and a smooth, knitted surface on the other. Other techniques yield a fabric that is furry on both sides. The variations are endless and new methods are being invented all the time. Most fleeces are made of polyester, so that they're quite similar in their rapid drying and retention of loft when wet. The differences are in appearance, softness, wind resistance, and resistance to pilling (the formation of little balls of fiber on the outside of the jacket, caused by abrasion).

Some fleece garments are made now that include a built-in wind-blocking layer. That's convenient when you want to throw on something warm to run some errands around town, but less versatile in the backcountry.

Fleece garments that contain a hood can be hard to find, but offer tremendous versatility. In cool weather, push the hood back and let excess heat escape from your neck and head. In cooler weather, pull up the hood. In frigid weather, add a synthetic ski hat on top of the hood to double-insulate your head, the most heat-loss-prone area of your body. For twenty years, I've made certain my outdoor wardrobe always contained a hooded fleece garment.

If fleece is so great, who needs a parka? The problem is that fleece offers relatively little loft for its weight compared to the insulation normally used to fill parkas. Fleece weighs several pounds per cubic foot, compared to half a pound per cubic foot for high-loft polyester battings, even less for high-quality down. When I expect severe cold, I always bring a parka.

CHOOSING A PARKA FILLING

Your first task when shopping for a parka is choosing the filling. Since you'll face the same choice in an even more important context when selecting a sleeping bag, I'll hit the subject lightly here and go into more detail in the chapter on sleeping bags.

High-quality down still provides more warmth for its weight than any synthetic insulation yet devised and it compresses into a smaller bundle. In addition, down is wonderfully soft, wrapping comfortably around your body in ways that the lower-grade synthetics can't begin to match. The garment's ability to hug your body as you move, referred to in the trade as its drape, also affects its warmth. A stiff garment allows pockets of air to form next to your body. When you move, that air is pumped out at the waist, neck, and cuffs—the forced convection I described earlier. Synthetics in general don't drape as well as down.

If you take good care of a down parka, it will retain its loft far longer than a synthetic one. Down is more expensive initially, but its greater durability can make it actually cheaper to own per year. However, if you find that you retire parkas after three or four years because the shell has become stained or ripped, then spending the money on a long-lasting fill may be a waste.

On the negative side, down, like cotton, loses all its resiliency when it gets wet. Data from Du Pont show that the insulation value of a Quallofil synthetic bag drops 15 percent when it has absorbed 25 percent of its weight in water. The insulation of a down bag drops 50 percent.

New synthetic insulations debut regularly with great fanfare. Some stand the test of time; others quietly vanish. Two names, however, have endured for many years and so are worth mentioning here.

PolarGuard, the iron horse of the synthetics, is a batting made of long, continuous strands of polyester. It has a well-established reputation for durability, and the newer (and more expensive) versions are softer and more compressible than the original. Quallofil, another synthetic with a long track record, is a batting made of short polyester fibers.

Both have the virtues of drying fast and retaining more of their insulation value when wet than down. Neither provides as much warmth for a given weight as top-quality down nor do they compress as well as down. If you want a synthetic parka because you need to save money or you'll be camping in a very damp climate, go to a specialty shop and find out what insulation is currently the top-dog in the synthetic insulation wars.

One solution to the problem of using down in a damp climate is to buy a down parka with a waterproof or water-resistant shell. That helps up to a point; in some situations, however, it's still pretty tough to keep down dry indefinitely. Sailing in foul weather and sea-kayaking and river-running, particularly in northern climates, are prime examples. So is backpacking in cold, dank climates like coastal Alaska. In those situations, your best efforts to stay dry usually mean getting wet more slowly. Synthetic parkas have the advantage that they lose less loft in perennially drizzly climates. However, the oft-repeated claim that "synthetics are warm when wet" needs qualification.

Professor W. C. Kaufman at the University of Wisconsin's Human Biology Department conducted a test in which he saturated a PolarGuard jacket and a down jacket by soaking and wringing them out repeatedly until they would hold no more water. Then he put the garments onto volunteers in a 40-degree room. Skin temperature readings were actually slightly lower for the PolarGuard than for the down. It's true that the PolarGuard did not collapse when wet, while the down did. The PolarGuard did indeed offer more resistance to heat loss by convection and conduction. However, the effect of evaporation completely overwhelmed any residual insulation provided by the PolarGuard. I would guess both garments felt quite chilly. The moral is that you must keep your insulation from getting soaked no matter what it's made of. A synthetic jacket is only better than a down one if it's merely damp, not if it's completely soaked.

My preference in parka insulation has been honed by my experiences in the wintertime Rockies and in the high, glaciated mountains of the Alaska Range. For those climates, which are very cold and relatively dry, I prefer down, particularly if protected by a water-resistant shell. In the wetter climate of the Northwest and Northeast, and in coastal Alaska and Canada, a synthetic-filled parka is probably a better bet.

THIN INSULATORS

There's a whole other class of "thin" insulators available that give about 60 to 80 percent more insulation for a given *thickness* than high-loft polyester battings. Thin insulations are made of microfibers only two to ten microns thick—much thinner than the 25-micron fibers used in high-loft battings. These insulations work so much better than high-loft battings on a thickness basis because their higher-than-average density serves as a better-than-average barrier to the loss of radiant heat. In addition, their fibers are the right size to effectively scatter the wavelengths of infrared radiation most commonly produced by the human body. Radiation must take a very circuitous path through a thin insulator before escaping.

The drawback of thin-fiber insulators is their greater density— their greater weight per unit of warmth. Thin-fiber insulations are useful where bulk is a drawback and weight is not critical. Gloves are one example; fashionable ski clothes are another. Some mountaineers in extremely cold environments, for example during the first winter ascent of McKinley's Cassin Ridge and an ascent of the Himalayan peak Cholatse, felt the bulk of the high-loft garments they would be forced to carry was so great that they preferred some extra weight to reduce the mummified feeling. In general, however, high-loft polyester insulations or down are more useful in the backcountry where weight is the prime concern.

WHAT TO LOOK FOR IN PARKA DESIGN

Regardless of the filling you choose, a good parka should reach below your buttocks to conserve the large amounts of heat produced by the muscles there. Parkas with elastic at the bottom hem tend to ride up to belt level, reducing their value. Better parkas have a storm skirt, a band of fabric that snaps around your waist to help prevent your movements from pumping out warm air. Most down parkas, even the good ones, have sewn-through seams: places where the inner and outer shells are sewn directly to each other, with no insulation in between. That's fine if the compartments are well filled with down. To compare the filling of different parkas, hold them up to a strong light.

Good hoods fasten easily, even with gloves on. Some are designed to cover your mouth; others fasten below your chin. I much prefer those that fasten below my chin so my breath doesn't condense in the insulation. Thoughtfully designed parkas also have differentially cut shoulder areas. The outer layer in the shoulders is cut larger than the inner layer, so the weight of the jacket is supported by the inner shell. This gives the insulation in the shoulder area room to expand. In jackets without this kind of cut, the shoulder area insulation is compressed by the jacket's weight.

My favorite sleeve design features knit cuffs recessed inside the end of the sleeve for protection from snow. Unprotected knit cuffs collect snow quickly. Elastic cuffs don't seal warm air in as effectively. Parkas with waterproof outer shell fabrics stay drier longer.

The best parka in the world won't keep you warm if it's saturated by rain or melting snow. The best fleece suit won't keep you warm if the wind is driving its icy fingers through every square inch. To stop the wind, rain, and snow, you need a good shell jacket and pants. That's what I'll consider next.

4

THE SHELL GAME: CLOTHING TO STOP WIND, RAIN, AND SNOW

Half-blinded by the driving sleet and rain, I thought for a moment I was watching Napoleon's retreat from Moscow. Hikers in an endless line snaked down the trail toward timberline 2,400 feet below. A few were well equipped, with snug rain jackets and waterproof pants. Far too many, however, were flatlanders unprepared for the vicious summer thunderstorms that plague Colorado's 14,256-foot Longs Peak. The frigid rain had already soaked most of them down to their cotton underwear. For them, a simple sprained ankle would have turned discomfort into serious trouble. Although the calendar said August, the temperature was in the low 40s. With the wind chill, it was well below freezing.

What those ill-prepared hikers needed was well-built shell clothing: uninsulated pants and jacket made of waterproof and windproof fabric. Shell gear that simultaneously "breathes"—releases sweat in the form of sweat vapor—while resisting wind and rain would have further increased their comfort.

Shell clothing is a critical part of any outdoor enthusiast's wardrobe. Clothing soaked by rain or melting snow will chill you faster than anything besides a dunking in a mountain lake. When the wind gets rowdy, even dry clothing should usually be covered by a windproof shell. Shells add significant warmth even in still air. Tests by REI showed that adding an uninsulated shell parka to a fleece jacket allowed the wearer to remain comfortable when the temperature in the test chamber was dropped eight degrees.

Staying warm and dry in a cold, steady rain demands good gear and a lot of savvy. In fact, it's often more difficult to stay warm in 33-degree rain than it is to stay warm in a snowstorm because rain will eventually penetrate the tiniest weakness in your shell gear. Snow won't.

WATERPROOF VERSUS WATER-RESISTANT

Before we go on, let's define a few terms. "Waterproof" fabrics will keep you dry in a tropical monsoon. "Water-resistant" fabrics resist the entry of drizzle and mist, at least for a time, but aren't designed to shed sustained, heavy rain. Their most common use is in cold-weather athletic apparel, where the athlete is more concerned about letting sweat vapor escape than about rain getting in. Water-resistant fabrics are usually much more breathable than waterproof fabrics.

The rule of thumb used to distinguish water-resistant from waterproof fabrics at the Army's Research Institute of Environmental Medicine in Natick, Massachusetts, is that a waterproof fabric should not leak when water exerts a force of 25 pounds per square inch. The Mullens Hydrostatic Test is the most common waterproofness test today.

If 25 psi seems like overkill, consider the pressure exerted on fabric when kneeling on wet ground. Consider, too, the pressure exerted by pack straps as a heavy load shifts back and forth. In addition, the initial performance of the fabric must be good enough so that no leakage occurs if the fabric is stretched when water pressure is applied. For its heavy-duty rain parka and trousers, Natick specifies that the fabric withstand 250 psi water pressure. Fabrics that waterproof can rival medieval armor in stiffness and aren't much more comfortable to wear.

The term "water-repellent" means the fabric causes water droplets to bead up on its surface. The term is confusing, because all waterproof *and* water-resistant fabrics are also given a water-repellent treatment to make water bead up. This water-repellent treatment is applied to the *outside* of the fabric and is completely distinct

---

from whatever coating or laminate is used on the *inside* to make the fabric waterproof or water-repellent. Later in the chapter I'll get into the importance of these DWR (durable water-repellent) treatments.

FABRICS FOR SHELL CLOTHING

Before selecting shell gear, decide how you're going to use it. If you primarily want a garment for an hour-long, cold-weather workout, consider buying a highly breathable but only water-repellent shell. During an intense workout you'll need all the breathability you can get. No highly breathable fabrics are truly waterproof. Fortunately, complete waterproofness is usually unnecessary during a brief workout.

If you're going to be exposed to the weather for more than an hour or so, such as on a long, cold hike or ski, then you'll want a totally waterproof shell, which implies sacrificing some breathability. That's usually an acceptable compromise because the lower-intensity, longer-duration activity should mean you'll be producing less sweat.

The least expensive shell gear is made of uncoated nylon with a DWR finish. Such gear is water-resistant, at least for a time, moderately wind-resistant, and breathable. That makes it a reasonable choice for short, intense, cold-weather workouts.

The next step up from simple uncoated nylon for those seeking a workout shell is one of the highly breathable "water-resistant-by-construction" fabrics. These "microfiber" fabrics are woven extremely tightly from very fine yarns, most often polyester, but sometimes a polyester/nylon blend.

These fabrics resist water better than ordinary uncoated nylon and breathe well enough to let most sweat escape during a hard run, but they aren't designed for use as rainwear. Their construction and DWR treatment will keep off mist and drizzle, but not a downpour. On the Mullens test, their water-resistance is usually one psi or less.

There are now a variety of other highly breathable, water-repellent, high-tech fabrics intended for aerobic sports where total waterproofness is unnecessary. Some of these expensive fabrics are modified waterproof/breathable fabrics where the manufacturer shifted the balance from truly waterproof/moderately breathable to water-resistant/highly breathable. Like all premium products, new (or supposedly new) versions are introduced regularly, with much fanfare. Rather than name names here and have you discover that my current favorite has gone the way of the Edsel by the time you read this, I'll let you explore the shelves of a good specialty retailer on your own for the latest and greatest.

Now let's talk about the shell gear you need for a daylong or multiday trip.

For several years, at the beginning of my outdoor career, I got away with using an uncoated nylon jacket and pants for wintertime trips in the cold, dry, climate of the Rockies. True, if I sat in the snow for any length of time, I got wet. In addition, the fabric wasn't as windproof as fabrics that are both waterproof and breathable.

High winds reduce the insulation provided by any clothing system by increasing convection at the outside surface and by forcing cold air through the outer shell. However, a very windproof fabric reduces the chilling effect of wind. If your shell is totally windproof, you're left with 20 to 40 percent more insulation in high winds than you'd have with a conventional nylon shell, according to W. L. Gore, maker of the first popular waterproof-breathable fabric, Gore-Tex.

My experience certainly confirms the value of a totally windproof shell. When I first started using a Gore-Tex jacket, I was convinced it didn't breathe simply because I got so hot in it while wearing the same number of layers I'd typically worn under my old uncoated nylon shell gear. Then I realized its windproofness was the cause. Removing one insulating layer stopped the overheating—and gave me one more insulating layer to hold in reserve for when the temperature really plummeted. If you can afford it, buy only waterproof/breathable shell gear for extended winter outings, whether in the Rockies or elsewhere.

Good shell gear is just as important in the summer as in the winter. For extended summer use, your shell gear must be reliably waterproof.

The least expensive truly waterproof garments are made of sheets of vinyl with heat-sealed seams. They're incredibly cheap and serve well for fetching the mail from your mailbox, but don't have the durability necessary for anything more adventurous.

The next step up in rainwear fabric intended for hiking and backpacking is urethane-coated nylon. These fabrics are waterproof, but don't breathe at all. These days, most hikers and backpackers choose one of the many waterproof-breathable fabrics available.

HOW WATERPROOF/BREATHABLE FABRICS WORK

All the waterproof-breathables currently available use either the microporosity principle or the absorbent-film principle. Both types of fabric work because of the difference between water as vapor and water as liquid.

Water droplets are composed of molecules held together by an attraction called the van der Waals force. Water vapor, on the other hand, is composed of single water molecules energetic enough to overcome the van der Waals force and bounce away from each other, forming a gas.

Microporous waterproof/breathable fabrics have pores big enough to permit single water molecules in vapor form to pass through. A water molecule is roughly .0002 microns across. The pores range from .2 to 2 or more microns, depending on the fabric. The pores are small enough, however, to prevent the passage of liquid water droplets so long as the microporous film or coating is hydrophobic—in other words, so long as drops of water tend to bead up on the microporous surface rather than wick through the holes.

Some microporous fabrics leak when contaminated by oils from your skin, insect repellent, soap residues, or sunscreen. These agents change the surface characteristics of the film or coating so that water tends to wick (just as it does along treated polypropylene and polyester) rather than bead up. The water eventually wicks through the holes, soaking the wearer.

Absorbent-film waterproof-breathables have no pores. Instead, the extremely water-loving film, which is .001 of an inch thick or less, absorbs water molecules on the hot, sweaty side, passes them through the film by diffusion and releases them on the cooler, drier side. In theory, no liquid water penetrates, even when the fabric gets contaminated, because no pores exist as little tunnels.

Gore-Tex originally worked solely on a microporosity principle. It was made of a sheet of polytetrafluoroethylene, better known by Du Pont's trademark, Teflon. The sheet was stretched to make it porous, then either laminated to one protective fabric, which became the jacket's outermost layer, or glued to two fabrics with the Gore-Tex in the middle. When W. L. Gore realized that contamination was causing leakage, they solved the problem by adding a non-porous absorbent film.

All types of waterproof/breathable fabrics need a good DWR (durable water-repellent) finish in order to breathe most effectively. This finish, which is distinct from the coating or membrane that makes the fabric waterproof, causes rain or melting snow to bead up and run off the surface of the fabric rather than spreading out in a thin film that evenly coats the fabric. When a fabric "wets out" (is coated completely with water), evaporation chills the fabric, which encourages condensation inside, reducing breathability. Unfortunately, most DWR finishes wear off after a few washings. Fortunately, there are now several good after-market products available that can restore your shell's water-repellency and hence its breathability. In my experience, they're well worth the trouble and expense of applying them.

THE LIMITATIONS OF WATERPROOF-BREATHABLE FABRICS

In theory, waterproof-breathable fabrics should create a hiker's nirvana. In practice, there are limitations. As one industry wag put it, "Gore-Tex is not an antiperspirant." He could have been referring to the other waterproof-breathables as well. To understand the limitations of these fabrics, we need to make a fast foray into physics.

The first limitation involves the force required to drive sweat in the form of water vapor through the fabric. Waterproof-breathable fabrics can't "pump out" water vapor. Nor do they work by permitting air to flow easily through the fabric, taking sweat vapor with it. In fact, all of these fabrics boast, rightfully, of their windproofness. Instead, water vapor moves through the fabric only when driven by a vapor pressure gradient.

Picture a closed box filled with water vapor but no air. The water molecules are bouncing off the box's walls and exerting a pressure, called the vapor pressure. Raise the temperature and the molecules get more excited. They bounce off the walls harder and more frequently, and the vapor pressure goes up. Cool the box, and the opposite happens: The vapor pressure drops.

Now add air to your imaginary box. *The vapor pressure exerted by the water molecules remains the same.* Warm the box, and the water vapor pressure goes up; cool it and the vapor pressure drops.

Now let's say you've got two boxes butted up against each other. Only a waterproof-breathable membrane separates them.

Water molecules are banging into and passing through the membrane from both sides, but the box with the greater vapor pressure (the warmer one) has more energetic water molecules, so more of them bang into the membrane and pass through it each second. A net flow of water molecules begins. The difference in vapor pressure between the two sides is called the vapor-pressure gradient.

Waterproof-breathable fabrics "breathe" only when the vapor pressure is greater inside the fabric than out. The greater the vapor pressure gradient, the more vapor passes through the membrane per hour. The vapor pressure gradient is greatest when the fabric is close to the heat source, your 90-degree skin, and when the air outside is cool and dry. If you're sweating inside the garment in a steamy Georgia thunderstorm when the temperature inside the garment and out is 90 degrees, and the relative humidity inside and out is 100 percent, no sweat vapor will escape at all.

The temperature difference between the air immediately inside a shell jacket and the outside air is roughly constant, regardless of the outside temperature, if the wearer's activity level is constant. In cold weather you need more clothing underneath the jacket than you do when it's warm, but that doesn't affect the temperature drop from the inside to the outside of the shell itself, disregarding the other insulation.

Here's an example. On a 70-degree fall afternoon, the temperature immediately inside your shell jacket might be 80 degrees—a difference of 10 degrees. On a 32-degree winter's day, the temperature immediately inside your jacket might be 42 degrees—again a difference of 10 degrees. In both cases your skin temperature, if you're comfortable, would be around 90 degrees. In winter, of course, you'd probably have several insulating layers between your skin and the jacket, while in the fall you'd have one or none.

Unfortunately, the vapor pressure gradient produced by that near-constant drop in temperature across the shell is *not* constant.

If it's 42 degrees just inside the jacket and 32 degrees outside, you've got less than half the vapor pressure gradient that you'd have if it was 80 degrees just inside the jacket and 70 degrees outside. That's assuming the relative humidity inside and out is 100 percent. If the outside humidity is lower, which it usually would be, the difference in vapor pressure gradients is even greater.

The bottom line is this: In cold weather you've got only one-fourth to one-half the "breathability" that you have when the temperature is mild. Since it's easy, even in warm weather, to produce more sweat than a waterproof-breathable fabric will pass, you can imagine how sweaty you can get in the cold if you don't regulate your temperature by removing insulating layers.

A further problem in cold environments is condensation within the insulation between your skin and the shell garment. If the temperature drop between skin and environment is steep enough, most of the sweat vapor will condense long before reaching the shell. To take just one example, if the temperature just inside your uninsulated shell jacket is 32 degrees, as it could easily be when the outside temperature is ten or 20 degrees colder, then roughly 85 percent of the moisture produced by your body will have condensed by the time it reaches the shell. Liquid water, of course, won't pass through any waterproof-breathable.

In real cold, the most breathable fabric in the world does little good. To gain some idea yourself of any waterproof-breathable fabric's limitations, pour boiling water into a jar. Cap the jar with a piece of fabric held on with a strong rubber band. Place the jar in the freezer. Within half an hour the inside of the fabric will be a sheet of ice.

Despite their limitations, waterproof-breathable fabrics do work better than purely waterproof, nonbreathable fabrics in many situations. I once conducted a test where I skied for an hour with a urethane-coated gaiter on one leg and a Gore-Tex gaiter on the other. At the end of the hour, the Gore-Tex gaiter had certainly trapped some condensation; the coated gaiter, however, had trapped far more. For more than twenty years, all of my shell clothing has been made of a waterproof-breathable fabric. But I still stop to strip down the moment I start to overheat.

Which waterproof-breathable is best? Even if I had the perfect answer for you today, the answer could change tomorrow. However, Gore-Tex certainly ranks at or near the top and has for many years. Competing products are generally less waterproof, less breathable, or both. As in most things, you get what you pay for. Some inexpensive waterproof-breathable fabrics are breathable in name only.

DURABILITY

No fabric remains waterproof forever. Coatings abrade and eventually leak. The glue dots holding the Gore-Tex membrane to its fabrics put stresses on the membrane when the fabric is flexed during use or when stuffed into a pack. Eventually, the membrane can get small tears and start to leak.

In general, the heavier the coating, the greater the durability. Some coated rainwear have a very light fabric laminated to the coating on the inside. This scrim, as it's called, should help reduce abrasion as well. Likewise, the heavier the fabric protecting the Gore-Tex membrane, the more durable it will be. The three-layer Gore-Tex laminates, where all layers are glued to each other, tend to be more durable than the two-layer versions with a free-floating liner, or the three-layer versions where the Gore-Tex is laminated only to a free-floating central layer. Don't take a running suit made of featherweight ripstop nylon to Everest, then expect to stay dry when you hike out through the monsoon afterward.

PONCHOS, CAGOULES, AND RAINSUITS

No material, no matter how waterproof, will keep you dry if it's sewn into a poorly designed and constructed garment.

For starters, forget about ponchos for winter use or serious rain. Ponchos are large, rectangular sheets of waterproof material with a hole in the center for your head. Most have hoods and are large enough to fit over a small pack. They offer good ventilation, low cost, and very few seams, which are always potential leak points. If the wind kicks up, however, you'd better sprint for your car. Wind lifts the bottom of the poncho, obscuring vision of your feet and letting wind-driven rain and snow soak you from the waist down. In addition, tree limbs have the same affinity for the flapping fabric that they do for Charlie Brown's kite.

Cagoules give somewhat better protection, but not by much. Cagoules are mid-calf or ankle-length, hooded, pullover garments with a short zipper at the neck. Though they have less tendency to lift in a wind, they still obscure your feet and often shorten your stride.

Far and away the best shell gear for cold, snowy, or rainy weather is a jacket and pants. I learned the hard way that pants are just as important as a jacket. While scrambling up Longs Peak one August day I made the mistake of ignoring the growing thunderhead rumbling directly toward me. I was at 14,000 feet when the storm struck. I donned my jacket and headed down as the fearsome updrafts roaring up the steep slopes swept freezing rain, hail, and snow into my face. The deluge immediately soaked my cotton-polyester pants. I'd put them on in the morning thinking, This is summer, right? No need for the full winter regalia. As I slid on my butt down ice-coated rocks, then started running for timberline, I swore I'd never venture into the high mountains again in any month without full protection.

Make sure your rain pants come down over the tops of your boots. If they stop short, water runs off your legs and turns your boots into bathtubs. If you end up with short pant legs for some reason, you can beat the runoff problem by wearing waterproof gaiters with your pant legs outside.

Rain pants usually have a short ankle zipper that is often backed by a triangular gusset of fabric. They usually won't fit over double boots (extra-warm boots composed of both a soft insulating inner boot and rigid plastic outer shell), which means you have to take off your boots to put on your rain pants. Shell pants for winter use or expeditions, on the other hand, should have full-length separating side zippers so that the pants can be put on over double boots, skis, or crampons and be ventilated from the waist down. Using pants intended mostly for snow in heavy rain can lead to leakage through the long zippers.

Here's what I look for in a shell jacket.

First off, I like shell jackets with full-length front zippers because they're easier to get on and off than pullover-style jackets. They're also easier to ventilate and provide better access to inside pockets. The most rain-worthy models have two storm flaps covering the front zipper. The inner flap is folded back on itself, forming a "gutter." Flaps that are held down with hook-and-loop are usually more watertight than those held with snaps. They are also much easier to manipulate with cold, wet fingers or gloves. Avoid storm flaps that constantly bind in the zipper.

Most high-quality jackets these days come with factory-sealed seams, in which a strip of seam tape is permanently glued on by heat and pressure. If your new jacket lacks factory-sealed seams, you'll have to seal them yourself. All hand-applied seam dopes require careful application and frequent renewal if you want to stay dry. Apply them when the fabric is stretched to open up the pinholes where the needle went through.

I like hoods that are big enough to accommodate a ski hat, yet have some provision for reducing their volume, usually via a hook-and-loop strap or drawcord found in back, when I'm not wearing a hat. Hoods that lack this feature tend to fall down in front and cover your eyes.

I prefer zippered pockets situated high on the jacket's front panel. They should be inside the pack shoulder straps, beneath the pack's sternum strap, and above the waist belt. Cargo pockets, usually found low on the jacket on either side of the zipper, are useful for hand-warming but not for carrying cargo. If you're carrying a pack, you'll find your hip belt completely blocks access to the pockets and jams the contents into your hips.

Cuffs should be cut wide for ventilation with the option of cinching the cuff closed with hook-and-loop so you can reach over your head and not have your sleeve turn into a downspout funneling water into your garment. Constantly closed knit or elastic cuffs inhibit ventilation too much.

Roomy rain jackets are easier to ventilate than tight ones because they pump out larger amounts of moist air when you move. In addition, they encourage a stronger "chimney effect," in which cool outside air enters at the waist, flows upward, and escapes at the neck, taking moist air with it. That can help reduce condensation.

Of course, if you're wearing a pack, the waist belt will stop any chimney-effect ventilation. In that case, try ventilating by opening the front zipper. I also try to ventilate by opening my "pit zips," long ventilating zippers that start near my elbow and run across my armpit to the bottom of my ribcage. Pit zips are a worthwhile feature found on better jackets. Unfortunately, both pit zips and the front zipper will let in snow and rain if it's really dumping. The best cooling system when you're wearing a pack in severe weather is simply to remove an insulating layer.

Manufacturers recognize, of course, that condensation can occur even inside a waterproof-breathable fabric. To combat condensation, some employ various kinds of lining fabrics intended to soak up the perspiration and spread it out through wicking so, at least in theory, it can escape more readily. Wicking in underwear is touted as a virtue for the same reason.

The fanciest of these lining fabrics are bicomponent, with a hydrophobic ("water-hating") layer inside, toward your skin, and a hydrophilic ("water-loving") layer outside. In theory the inner layer always feels dry while the outer layer wicks very fast. Although these liners have some virtues, particularly in mild weather, they also add bulk and cost. I try to avoid sweating hard enough to give them a chance to do their job.

When trying on shell jackets, put on a loaded pack, fasten the hip belt, and lift your arms. Some shoulder/sleeve designs give you more freedom of movement than others. Try touching your elbows together in front of you to check for freedom in that movement. Can you reach forward without the sleeves pulling up and exposing clothing beneath?

USING YOUR SHELL GEAR

Raingear adds a lot of warmth to your clothing system. Hikers on rainy days often face a dilemma: Do they want to get soaked by rain or by sweat? If they leave the raingear in their pack, they get soaked by cold rain—obviously a bad choice. But if they add their raingear on top of everything else, they sweat hard. Condensation inside the raingear, caused by sweat vapor hitting the cold, rain-chilled shell fabric, quickly soaks their insulation. Rain-suited hikers tend to overheat while moving and quickly become chilled when they stop.

As a first step toward solving the problem, consider removing an insulating layer before putting on your raingear, rather than adding the raingear on top of everything else. If you can't bring yourself to do that, then pause to remove clothing at the first sign of overheating.

For sustained rainy hiking in the summer I often strip down to nylon shorts and a synthetic T-shirt, then put my raingear on directly over that. To be sure, the raingear feels a bit clammy right next to my skin. Wearing such little insulation usually means I have to keep moving steadily to stay warm, taking only brief breaks to wolf down a granola bar and some water, but I can avoid overheating and soaking my insulating layers with sweat that way. As soon as I get to camp, I pitch my tent, crawl inside, strip off that dank raingear and put on all the dry insulating layers I've been carrying in my pack. What little sweat has accumulated in my T-shirt and shorts quickly dries, and within minutes I'm completely comfortable once more.

Even the best hoods tend to remain stationary when you turn your head. Result: a stunning view of the inside of your hood. Winter solution: Wear goggles over the hood to keep the hood in place when you turn your head. Summer solution: Wear a synthetic baseball cap under your hood. The brim forces the hood to turn with your head. It also shields your glasses from rain.

One final thought: Don't come home from a trip and cram your wet raingear into an airless closet while it's wet. The combination of heat and moisture will encourage the growth of mildew, which is not only ugly, but can also render your urethane-coated raingear porous. For that matter, don't store any gear while it's wet. Upon your return home, your first task should be to spread out all of your wet gear—clothing, tent, sleeping bag, etc.—and let it dry thoroughly before putting it away in a cool, dry place.

ONLY THIRTY
DOLLARS PER TOE:
THE SECRETS OF
WARM FEET

After a week of 20-below weather, Tom Reid figured Upper Titcomb Lake, in Wyoming's Wind River Range, would be frozen solid. He figured wrong. Flowing water near the lake's outlet had kept the ice thin. Without warning, the ice shattered beneath his skis.

He threw himself backward and landed on solid ice, soaked to his knees. Instantly his clothes turned to ice. He sprinted for the snow cave some skiers had built four miles away. Luckily, he arrived unscathed.

That night he dried his wet socks and low-cut touring boots in his sleeping bag. By morning only the boots felt damp. He decided to ski to his car, eighteen miles away.

After five miles of skiing, with the temperature at 25 below, the molded plastic soles of his boots cracked and began to fall apart. Snow crept inside, melted, then froze. Still, he thought he could reach his car without frostbite. He hurried on.

Just before sunset his toes went numb. At eight P.M. he reached his car. Six toes felt like marble. Within hours they blistered black. Not even prompt medical attention could repair the damage. Two months later he honed the tip of his friend's sharpest buck knife and severed the last scrap of dead flesh holding on what had once been the two smallest toes of his right foot.

Good footwear may seem expensive at first glance. High-quality double boots for skiing and mountaineering cost three-hundred dollars and up. Still, as veteran boot repairman Steve Komito puts it, "Good boots are actually cheap. They cost only thirty dollars per toe."

Don't pay cheap footwear's true price. Good boots pay for themselves in the long run.

The first step in selecting cold-weather footwear is to figure out what terrain you'll be encountering, the temperatures you're likely to meet, and how you plan to get around. Hikers need a boot that flexes at the ball of the foot; mountaineers wearing crampons want one that doesn't. Skiers need a boot that fits their bindings and is stiff enough to provide edge control. Lightly laden snowshoers need warmth, primarily; they need warmth plus support if they're carrying a heavy load.

You also need to learn, from experience, how much insulation you need. Some people are apparently born with sluggish circulation in their toes. Others have abused their feet in the past by letting them go numb repeatedly, which slowly but surely damages the foot's circulatory system. My friend Janet spent her teenage years ski-racing in tight boots she'd cranked down to the limit for better control. Her feet had been constantly numb. The bad habit bit back when we went to McKinley in April in identical boots with identical socks. My feet (I grew up surfing in Southern California) were fine; hers were always painfully cold.

BOOTS FOR COLD-WEATHER HIKING

In moderate cold, when the ground is dry, ordinary fabric/leather or all-leather hiking boots can be sufficient. Buy them big enough to fit properly with two pairs of socks, one thin, one thick.

Once there's snow on the ground, you need to worry about keeping your feet dry. Fabric/leather boots have lots of seams, which makes them prone to leaks, and you can't use ordinary boot waterproofings on the fabric. All-leather boots, particularly those with a "one-piece" upper, have fewer seams and are easier to keep waterproof.

Split leather is a layer of hide that doesn't contain the skin surface, called the grain. Splits are usually weaker and less water-proof than full-grain leathers containing the skin surface. Almost all fabric/leather boots use pieces of split leather. Heavy-duty boots generally use full-grain leather for its durability and water resistance. Good leather is expensive, so price is a pretty good indication of quality.

Leaky boots chill your feet as much as leaky raingear chills the rest of you. Many boot manufacturers today claim that the leather they use in their top-quality boots will remain waterproof for the life of the boot. In my experience, however, even the best boots begin to leak after a few seasons. Once that cold, wet, squishy feeling starts to develop around your toes, it's time to give your boots a little TLC.

Start by cleaning your boots with warm water and a scrub brush. Mud left on a boot will work its way into the stitching. As you walk or ski, the boot's flexing will grind up the thread. Then dry your boots at room temperature. Never let leather boots get hotter than your own skin can tolerate. Heat damages leather, and can also delaminate the sole.

Next, apply a reasonable amount of boot conditioner. Here controversy reigns, with each manufacturer of conditioner finding some reason to claim that rival products will rot the leather, degrade the stitching, and delaminate the soles as well as give you night sweats and premature baldness. The safest course is to use the conditioner recommended by the boot manufacturer (if the manufacturer recommends one), if for no other reason than to preserve your rights under the warranty. Mink oil and neat's-foot oil are intended to soften leather that has become hard and brittle; they should not be used as waterproofing agents.

Don't lather on any boot conditioner. Your boots will turn into dishrags. In addition, the extra gunk will collect dirt, particularly along the welt, which will wear on the stitching.

W. L. Gore makes a Gore-Tex boot liner for fabric/leather and all-leather boots out of a membrane that's supposed to be twice as thick and four times as tough as the apparel membrane. In my experience, a Gore-Tex lining makes boots reliably waterproof for several seasons of hard use. If you do a lot of hiking in wet, moderately cold conditions, a pair of Gore-Tex boots may be just right. Boots take a lot of punishment, however, so don't expect a membrane only .002 inches thick to remain waterproof forever.

BOOTS FOR SKIING

Once the snow is too deep for easy walking, you'll need to travel on either skis or snowshoes.

In my opinion, skis are toys for having fun. Snowshoes are tools for hauling loads. Trying to ski with 60 pounds of winter camping gear on your back is an exercise in masochism. In that situation, snowshoes, particularly in steep, dense timber, can actually be faster. They're certainly safer (less risk of tearing up your knees) and are much less frustrating. Get your ski tips tangled and that 60-pound monkey on your back will smash your face into the snow and refuse to let you up. Snowshoers rarely make that kind of mistake.

Don't get me wrong: I love to ski, and when I'm traveling lightly laden in the winter, I'm always on the long boards.

Light-duty backcountry ski boots are still made of leather, usually with a little insulation. Look for a full-grain upper and enough height and stiffness to give you some control over your skis. Such boots are fine for moderate cold and for gentle ski tours through the woods.

In severe cold, you need a ski boot with more insulation. You can't keep adding socks inside the same boot, however, because you quickly begin to constrict circulation in your feet. That's worse than having fewer socks. George Leigh Mallory reputedly once stopped high on Everest to remove a pair of socks so his feet could warm up. You also can't just buy a bigger boot and add more socks, beyond a certain point, because the socks compress too much. Your foot walks around inside the boot instead of outside, and you lose all control. You need more insulation, but in a form that won't compress readily. You need a double boot.

Double boots are just that: a soft, insulated inner boot and a rugged, usually uninsulated, outer shell. In years past, skiers expecting serious cold could buy leather double boots. These days leather double boots have vanished, to be replaced by plastic double boots. These boots have a soft fabric-and-foam inner boot and a stiff plastic shell.

Plastic double boots for backcountry skiing come in two flavors. Telemark boots, named after the type of turn most skiers execute using that type of boot, are designed to be used with bindings that clamp the boot only at the toe. Alpine-touring boots resemble alpine ski boots. They're designed to fit bindings that let you lock your heel down for skiing downhill and free your heel for touring uphill. Both telemark and alpine-touring boots are much stiffer than any leather boot made, so they allow you to ski much better.

There's no room in a book on staying warm to go into the debate over telemark versus alpine-touring equipment. Both kinds of boots are equally warm. And, most important, both are much warmer than any leather single boot. If you love to ski, want maximum control, and want to go out in any kind of weather without worrying about frostbite, you'll eventually want a pair of double ski boots of one flavor or the other.

BOOTS FOR SNOWSHOEING

Almost any kind of boot will fit a snowshoe binding. Your summer hiking boots will probably be just fine for a quick snowshoe jaunt on a warm winter's day. For colder days and longer trips, you'll want either pac boots or what I'll call winter hiking boots.

Pac boots have an all-leather or leather and fabric upper stitched to a molded rubber bottom. A removable liner, usually made of wool or polypropylene felt, provides insulation. Wool liners cost less; polypro liners dry faster. For equivalent thickness, the warmth is about the same. Pac boots are warmer than winter hiking boots—sometimes too warm—and totally waterproof up to the top of the molded rubber. They're water-resistant above that. Pac boots are instantly comfortable, requiring no break-in time, but the fit is usually rather amorphous because the insulation compresses under your foot and the boots are normally available only in full sizes. When fitting a pair, make sure the top edge of the molded rubber doesn't jab you under the ankle bone while traversing a slope.

Pac boots are perfect for aurora watching and other inactive pursuits. For snowshoeing in rough terrain where you want a snugger fit and better ankle support, look for a pair of insulated, waterproof winter hiking boots. They'll lighten your wallet more than pac boots, but also lighten the load on your feet.

Many of these boots are marketed as hunting boots because they're targeted to the hook-and-bullet crowd, but don't let the name put you off. Hunters spend a lot of time walking off-trail in cold, snowy, or marshy terrain, and they need warm, waterproof footwear more than most backpackers.

Cold-weather hiking boots have all-leather or fabric and leather uppers that are stitched, cemented, or attached via injection molding to a stout lugged sole. All three construction techniques, including injection molding, which has been much improved in recent years, produce a durable boot. All-leather uppers typically cost more, weigh more, and last longer.

The insulation, which is stitched permanently into the boot lining, is usually Thinsulate, a microfiber batting that resists compression and provides a lot of warmth with minimum thickness. Some manufacturers use various closed-cell foams as insulation, which don't provide quite as much warmth as Thinsulate for equivalent thickness. As with summer hiking boots, the best insulated winter hiking boots back up their leather with a sewn-in Gore-Tex bootie.

For serious load-hauling on snowshoes, you may want to invest in a pair of mountaineering double boots, which I'll describe next.

WINTER AND HIGH-ALTITUDE MOUNTAINEERING BOOTS

Plastic double boots are the only choice for cold-weather mountaineering. Like plastic double boots for skiing, mountaineering double boots have a soft, insulated inner boot and stiff outer shell. They're designed to fit crampons and don't work in most ski bindings. Although plastic double boots seem incredibly tough, a few of the outer shells have cracked. You can't repair a cracked shell in the field (or in the repair shop, for that matter). All you can do is tape up the gap and head for home.

FITTING BOOTS

The best boot around isn't worth its weight in shoelaces if it doesn't fit. Boot repairman Steve Komito stresses, "A boot should feel good even when it's new. So often people are given the idea that they should wear a boot through suffering and pain and somewhere in the golden future it will feel good. I honestly don't feel that's necessary. The most critical point is adequate room in the toes, particularly for walking downhill. The boot has to keep your toes out of the toe box. The heel has to fit so there isn't excessive slipping. I suggest people lace up their boots snugly and walk. If there's heat after fifteen or twenty minutes, there's friction, and if there's friction, there are going to be blisters."

Boots are made on a last, a metal form that defines the shape of the boot. Different manufacturers use different lasts, some narrow, some wide, depending on what they think will fit the greatest number of feet. A few manufacturers offer different widths in the same size and model of boot. Don't accept the first pair that feels vaguely right. Try different models and different manufacturers, and even different stores, which may carry styles the first did not. Unlace the boot completely and shove your foot as far forward as possible, until your toes touch the front of the boot. If you can easily fit one finger in between your heel and the back of the boot, the length is about right. Lace up the boot and walk. Does your heel shift up and down inside the boot? A small amount of movement may be acceptable, particularly in a stiff, new boot. If the movement is excessive, however, it will cause blisters. Look for enough room at the front of the boot to "play piano with your toes." Snug boots restrict circulation, which can lead to cold feet, even frostbite.

If you're planning to carry a substantial load, try the boots on while wearing a pack. Stand on a sharp edge to test the arch support. Squat down and see if the toe box folds into a sharp wrinkle that jabs your toes. Let your foot roll to the side and see if the boot provides adequate ankle support. Unfortunately, the stiffer the boot, the harder it is to judge if it will be comfortable over the long haul. Be sure to wear your new boots around your house for several hours before taking them outside. Most good shops will let you return boots a few days after purchase if you've only worn them indoors.

SOCKS

Different sock combinations make a big difference in the way boots fit, so pick your socks before trying on boots. For cold weather, start with a thin synthetic sock. Then add a vapor-barrier sock, if you need one, then your insulating sock. Here wool clings to its last foothold, so to speak, in my stock of outdoor gear, mostly because I haven't yet found a thick, compression-resistant, 100-percent-synthetic sock. The best wool and wool blend socks cost twice as much as the cheap ones and last three times as long. The cheap ones wear away to their nylon reinforcement faster than you can say fishnet underwear.

If you can find them, buy socks that come in sizes, without elastic, rather than stretch ones. Wearing too many stretch socks can constrict circulation and lead to cold feet. Stretch socks don't last as well, either, because they stretch most, and so are thinnest, at the greatest wear points: your heel and toes.

Some climbers have experimented with using neoprene wet-suit booties as socks. The closed-cell foam provides good insulation and also acts as a vapor barrier. That means that the same foot-care procedures I described earlier for cloth vapor-barrier socks are imperative with neoprene socks. An additional danger may threaten high-altitude mountaineers using these socks. The gas inside the closed bubbles of the neoprene can expand as the air pressure outside drops with increasing altitude. That could cause the socks themselves to expand and reduce circulation, increasing the risk of frostbite.

GETTING THE MOST FROM YOUR WINTER BOOTS

Putting on cold boots is often like putting your feet in a bucket of ice water: Your feet get cold rather than your boots getting warm. The best solution is to sleep in your inner boots, leaving the shells at the foot of the tent.

In severe cold, putting on your boots every morning can start to seem like a hassle. My companions on Mt. Hunter's south face "solved" the problem by sleeping with their boots on for most of the climb. That proved to be a mistake. Your boots, socks, and feet all need to dry out after a day of hard work. In addition, it's hard to get every last ball of snow off your boots without taking your boots off. Any snow you miss melts and soaks your sleeping bag. Toward the end of the climb, my companions' bags had become nylon sheets enclosing clumps of frozen down—not a pleasant sight when you're facing a minus-20-degree night. Their damp socks provided little insulation. When we finally got off the climb after a grueling thirteen days, both checked into Providence Hospital with frozen feet.

GAITERS

If you're going to be wading through deep snow, you need some way to keep snow out of your boot tops. The cheapest, lightest way is a pair of gaiters, simple fabric tubes that cover most of your boot and reach up to your knee. A strap under the arch of your foot holds them down; a zipper lets you put them on over your boots. That zipper takes a lot of abuse, so make sure it's sturdy. Better gaiters have a storm flap that folds over the zipper and is held down with hook-and-loop. Snaps freeze shut fiercely in the damp environment where gaiters live. Avoid them when you can.

Not even the best mountaineering and skiing double boots, as they come off the shelf, will keep your feet warm at high altitude when it's way below zero. In most boots you can put a closed-cell foam insole between the outer and inner boots. In some you can also replace the wimpy inner-boot insole with something thicker and warmer. Plastic double boots in particular have very thin soles, increasing heat loss through the bottom of your feet. Be sure that adding insoles doesn't make your boots fit so tightly they constrict circulation.

If you've still got cold feet after inserting insoles, you need to add insulation outside the boot.

Supergaiters cover the entire boot down to the welt, but leave the sole free. That's an advantage for mountaineers who want to climb difficult rock, and for skiers who need their boot soles free to get into their bindings. Most supergaiters come with foam or synthetic-fiber insulation. They normally remain attached to your boots for the duration of your trip.

The disadvantage of supergaiters is that they leave a large surface area, your boot sole, in contact with cold, conductive snow or even colder and more conductive crampons. Overboots enclose the entire boot, including the sole. That means you either climb rock with your crampons on, or take your overboots off. It also means you'll have trouble getting your boot attached to your crampons and skis. In some cases, you can modify the overboots to work. In other cases, particularly with alpine ski bindings, you probably can't. But you do have the warmest boot setup you can get and still have a stiff boot somewhere inside. Few people really need overboots, so few companies make them. Try calling specialty mountaineering shops and asking them for sources.

If double boots with vapor-barrier socks, extra foam insoles, and overboots don't keep your feet warm, you've either cold-damaged your feet somewhere along the line, or you aren't maintaining your body. Body maintenance, in fact, is just as important as gear in preventing frostbite. I'll talk more about that in an upcoming chapter.

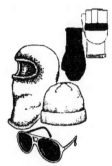

THE OUTERMOST NECESSITIES: GLOVES, HATS, GOGGLES, AND FACE MASKS

My two friends and I knew we had to move fast to get up the south face of Alaska's Mt. Hunter with the limited food we could carry. We left behind everything we deemed non-essential. That meant I left behind an extra pair of the nylon shell mittens called overmitts. After all, I was starting with a brand-new pair. One brand-new pair should last for ten days, right?

On the first day we began climbing snow-covered rock, which required tediously clearing each hold of snow. The constant abrasion began to wear on my overmitts. Swinging my ice axe for hours on end accelerated the deterioration. By the ninth day, gaping holes had appeared in the palms. Snow crept inside. Completely preoccupied by the struggle to ascend difficult ice in a 50-mph, sub-zero wind, I neglected my hands. By the day's end, all of my fingers and both thumbs had been severely frostbitten. I ended up losing the tips of three fingers.

It doesn't take an Alaskan epic to destroy or lose a pair of mittens or gloves. Lose control of one for just an instant in a high wind and it's gone. That's happened to me twice: once in a 100-mph gale in Rocky Mountain National Park, and once in a much milder wind that blew an overmitt over a huge cornice and down a potential avalanche path.

As I learned the hard way, it's critical to train yourself to always stow your gloves and mittens in a secure place as soon as you remove them for any reason. The best place is usually a zippered jacket or pack pocket. Second best is setting them on the ground with something heavy on them. Beware of gusty winds filling them with blowing snow.

On steep, difficult climbs, it's often inconvenient to put your hand protection in a pocket every time you need to fiddle with something with bare hands. In those situations, I often attach idiot strings to my overmitts even though they make me feel like my mother just bundled me up to walk to kindergarten.

The best system, in my opinion, is to tie a loop big enough for your head in the middle of a string connecting the overmitts. I put the loop over my head last, above all my garments including my hood. Then I put my pack on, followed by my overmitts. The crux is remembering to remove your overmitts and let them hang before taking your pack off. Idiot strings let you jerk your overmitts off and let them dangle when you're in a hurry to slam in that next ice screw.

This system isn't perfect, because blowing snow tends to fill your overmitts when they're dangling by your knees. You can prevent that, at least in part, by snugging down whatever closure exists at the end of the cuff.

You may find you prefer a different approach. Some people run a string between the two overmitts, put on the overmitts, then put on their shell jacket so the string runs up one sleeve, across the back and down the other sleeve. That keeps the string out of your way, but holds the overmitts close to your wrists, which makes it cumbersome to reach into a pocket or your pack.

Some overmitts and heavy gloves come with small elastic loops, which slip over the wearer's wrists. Other people attach their overmitts to their sleeves with small clips. When you need to shed your overmitts for a moment, you let them dangle from your wrist. These approaches have the same virtues and weaknesses as the string-through-the-sleeve approach.

Yet another approach is to keep some kind of spring-loaded clip attached to one of the D-rings commonly found on most pack shoulder straps. I snap a loop on my overmitts into the clip when the overmitts aren't in use. The clip I use is a carabiner, a three-inch-

THE BEST IDIOT-STRING ARRANGEMENT HAS A LONG CORD
CONNECTING THE TWO OVERMITTS WITH A LOOP TIED IN THE
MIDDLE TO FIT OVER THE WEARER'S HEAD.

long oval aluminum ring with a spring-loaded gate in one side. I use it because it's big enough to manipulate with gloves on. The clip-on system works well if you can take the time to clip and unclip your overmitts.

In addition to guarding my hand protection like it was the crown jewels, I also bring spares. Depending on the length and severity of the trip, that can mean not only spare overmitts, but spare gloves and mittens as well. I joke with my friends that the stuff sack containing my extra hand protection is as big as my sleeping-bag stuff sack, but I bring it nonetheless. Wintertime trekkers constantly handle snowy objects, which means gloves and mittens get wet quickly. Having spares can make all the difference in comfort.

On expeditions, I also carry yarn and a darning needle to patch thin spots in wool gloves and socks. I carry strong sewing thread and a thinner needle to stitch together small holes in lighter gloves.

It makes sense to layer your hands for the same reasons you layer your body: precise fine-tuning of insulation for different temperatures, extra warmth through air trapped between layers, and the ability to adjust your level of protection so your hands don't sweat and soak your gloves or mittens. With hand protection, there's an additional reason: Layering means you can separate the layers for fast drying on long trips. Wet gloves and mittens won't dry if you stick them in your pack. You either have to put them deep inside your clothing and leave them there, preferably overnight, or conjure up a hot, sunny day.

I start my layering system with light gloves that give me enough dexterity I almost never need to remove them. My favorite light gloves incorporate a windproof, water-resistant, and highly breathable membrane in between two very thin fleece layers. This membrane is the same material that makes my favorite aerobic running shell work so well. Although they're expensive, these gloves give me a better combination of dexterity and warmth than any other lightweight glove I've tried. On warmer days, these gloves are often the only ones I need. Since the outer fleece surface gets wet easily, I always carry two pairs.

As the temperature drops, I substitute a pair of heavier gloves for the light ones. My current favorite heavy gloves have a nylon-and-leather outer shell, a seam-sealed Gore-Tex lining, and synthetic insulation that dries quickly. Gloves this good may seem outrageously expensive—they cost as much as a decent pair of day-hiking boots—but to me they're worth it.

In temperatures down to about zero, that's all I need. However, I always carry a pair of heavily insulated mittens that have a nylon outer shell and a fleece lining. These mittens are big enough that I can wear them over my light fleece gloves in truly bitter cold. They also serve as a backup in case I lose one of my warm gloves. The fleece lining is removable for quick drying.

In really bitter cold, such as on big Alaskan climbs in the spring, when nighttime temperatures can hit 40 below, I substitute a pair of heavy knitted wool gloves for my light fleece gloves, then put an oversize pair of insulated overmitts on top. This combination was warm enough to keep me from getting frostbite again during a May ascent of Mt. McKinley two years after my Mt. Hunter epic. (My fancy Gore-Tex gloves are just too bulky to fit underneath the largest overmitt made.)

If you have chronic trouble with cold fingers, consider carrying mittens rather than gloves. Mittens are inherently warmer than gloves because they have less surface area in proportion to their volume. Every square inch of surface provides an opportunity for heat loss by radiation, convection, and conduction. Minimizing surface area also minimizes heat loss. The disadvantage of mittens, of course, is their lack of dexterity.

I dislike the insulated leather and fabric gloves used by downhill skiers because they lack a gauntlet, a long cuff that reaches up your forearm and closes the gap between your shell jacket's cuff and your hand protection. A friend once had his wrist severely frostbitten while ice-climbing in Huntington's Ravine on Mt. Washington simply because his hand protection didn't include an adequate gauntlet.

Any kind of glove or mitten with a gauntlet needs some kind of closure at the cuff to keep snow out and warm air in. Look for closures that are easy to adjust, even with an overmitt on the other hand.

Before you actually buy all the separate pieces of your hand layering system, make sure they fit together. Some insulated overmitts will only accommodate a thin liner glove inside. Trying to fit a heavy wool glove or mitten inside can force you to buy a larger size—which sometimes means the overmitt's finger section is way too long.

One other precaution before you buy sewn (as opposed to knitted) hand protection: If you can, turn the glove or mitten inside out and inspect the seams. Glove-makers use very narrow seam allowances, which means that a small sewing mistake creates a seam waiting to blow out. It's also a good idea to turn every sewn glove and overmitt inside out for an inspection before a long trip.

HATS

Layering applies as much to your head as to your hands. For starters, it's a good idea to have some way to cover your neck, which is just as well supplied with blood as your head and loses heat just as fast. A scarf works fine for sleigh rides on snowy evenings, but it's more cumbersome to use in the woods than several other solutions.

As I mentioned in the chapter on insulating layers, I like fleece garments with hoods. I also carry a fleece ski hat, which I can layer on top of the fleece hood in biting cold, or wear by itself if the temperature moderates.

If you can't find a hooded fleece sweater, consider carrying a balaclava. Balaclavas are knitted or fleece hats that cover everything from your shoulders up except for a circle surrounding your eyes, nose, and mouth. They were named after Balaclava, the Russian seaport on the Black Sea where the English cavalry made the ill-fated attack celebrated in "The Charge of the Light Brigade."

If you find balaclavas too claustrophobic, consider a neck gaiter, a simple fleece tube worn around your neck. Used in conjunction with a fleece ski, a neck gaiter gives you excellent versatility in layering.

Bomber hats are yet another good option. These hats look like fleece-lined, water-repellent baseball caps. They usually have long, fleece-lined flaps that wrap around your chin and secure with hook-and-loop when it's cold. The flaps can be folded over the top of the hat and secured by hook-and-loop when it's warmer.

For wet spring snow and cold rain, I like wearing an uninsulated Gore-Tex baseball cap because it keeps my hair dry (okay, so there's not *that* much hair left) and still lets some sweat vapor escape. Hair absorbs a lot of water; evaporation of that water robs you of heat, so it pays to keep your hair dry.

GOGGLES AND FACE MASKS

A balaclava alone will not keep your face from freezing when the wind is sandpapering your skin with blowing snow. A good pair of ski goggles helps a great deal. Buy the double-pane variety. Although they are usually more fragile, they often ice up less from condensation inside than the single-pane ones. Most goggles come with amber lenses that are supposed to enhance your ability to see terrain features clearly in flat light. For night travel, a clear lens is a better choice. If you try using an amber lens at night, you'll find that even the brightest headlamp seems too dim. Wearing prescription glasses inside goggles is usually a prescription for foggy vision. The best solution I've found is a pair of prescription goggles. Ask at a good optician or specialty ski shop for sources.

Goggles still leave the tip of your nose, chin, and lower cheeks exposed. For those really ugly days when you can't even look into the wind and secretly wish you were windsurfing in Tahiti, you need a face mask. I like the neoprene variety, which fits neatly under the lower edge of my goggles and covers every last scrap of flesh left exposed by the hood of my fleece sweater. Neoprene face masks stop the wind completely, unlike the thin knitted "face masks" that are actually shaped like balaclavas. Breathing through a fabric face mask quickly causes it to ice up. Face masks made of neoprene offer enough insulation to ice up less.

With a balaclava or fleece hood, goggles, and face mask, you can stare the worst snow-laden gale in the face and laugh—so long as it doesn't simply knock you flat, that is. I had always regarded face masks as too claustrophobic for extended use until three friends and I embarked on a 100-mile ski tour from the ski resort of Eldora, in Colorado's Front Range, to Vail. The first day we spent five hours above timberline on the Continental Divide, struggling through a horrendous gale. Without full face armor, we would either have turned back or risked freezing our cheeks. With it, we were able to find our way by map, compass, and altimeter through the blinding storm. Six days later, we arrived in Vail.

7

EIGHT INCHES OF HEAVEN: HOW TO SLEEP COMFORTABLY IN THE COLD

For three days, George Lowe, Lito Tejada-Flores, and Chris Jones had struggled with the steep rock on the south face of Devils Thumb, in the Coast Range near Petersburg, Alaska. Then the weather went sour. The storm began as cold rain. As the temperature dropped, the rain turned to sleet, then snow. Ice coated everything, including their garments. The loft of Tejada-Flores's down jacket shriveled to nothing as water saturated the down. Lowe remembers stuffing his fiberfill sleeping bag in the morning and seeing water ooze out. When he pulled it out in the evening, he could feel clumps of ice. Nonetheless, he stayed warm—at least, warm enough to survive.

"Without fiberfill bags, we simply couldn't have done it, or we would have died," Lowe says. "It's important for people to realize that in that climate, down is useless."

DOWN VS. SYNTHETIC, ROUND TWO

In coastal Alaska, Lowe is certainly right: Synthetic sleeping bags rule. On colder, higher peaks, the opposite is true: Down rules, particularly if it's protected by a water-resistant or waterproof shell, and particularly if you take the time to dry it at every available opportunity. To keep our down bags dry on long climbs in Alaska, we would get up at three or four A.M., climb until three P.M., then camp. Our yellow tent would become a greenhouse, drying our bags completely so we could sleep warm during the minus-20- to minus-40- degree night that would follow. The habit of drying his bag whenever possible became so ingrained in Peter Metcalf that the first thing he did after we checked into a motel following our Mt. Hunter climb was yank his sodden bag out of its stuff sack and begin to dry it. Synthetic bags should be dried whenever possible, too.

I discussed the basic differences between down and its synthetic competitors in the chapter on insulating clothing. Here's a quick refresher:

Down's advantages are:
- Greater warmth for weight, which means a 10 to 20 percent weight savings compared to a synthetic bag of comparable warmth
- Greater compressibility, which means less bulk in your pack
- Greater durability

Synthetic's advantages are:
- Greater warmth when wet
- Lower initial cost (though not necessarily lower cost per year of use)

Synthetic fiber manufacturers constantly improve their products and introduce new ones. The time may come when a synthetic can match down's warmth-for-weight, compressibility, and longevity. When it does, the synthetic will probably become the clear choice.

If you want a synthetic bag, your choices now in quality bags are the same as in parkas: PolarGuard or Quallofil. Bag makers vary in how they use the products, however, and the products keep evolving, so you'll have to do some research to decide which synthetic is actually best when you're ready to buy. A good specialty retail shop should know which synthetic is currently top dog.

THE LOWDOWN ON DOWN

If you choose down, you need to consider down quality. Down fill power is measured by putting one ounce of down into a graduated cylinder and dropping in a light weight called a platen. The down's fill power is the volume of the cylinder below the platen, measured in cubic inches per ounce of down. Price, compressibility, and loft for weight are all proportional to fill power.

Pretty good down lofts 550 cubic inches per ounce. Better down averages 650. The best down currently advertised for use in sleeping bags lofts 800 cubic inches per ounce. According to some reports, down from the eider duck can loft 1,200 cubic inches. That gossamer stuff comes only from far northern Europe and Iceland, where only a few thousand pounds are collected each year from the nests of wild eider ducks. Eider down costs something like six-hundred dollars a pound at wholesale. A simple eider down comforter will set you back a couple of grand.

Returning now from the stratosphere, how much difference does down quality make? On a full-blown, keep-you-warm-when-hell's-freezing-over expedition bag rated to minus-40, using 650 fill instead of 550 fill saves you about seven ounces. Using 800 fill instead of 550 saves another seven ounces. If you're intent on cutting ounces and cubic inches before embarking on some desperate climb, that might be significant to you. A better reason to seek out high-quality down is that any company using such a premium product is probably building excellent bags.

By FTC regulation, a sleeping bag advertised as containing "100 percent down" must indeed contain nothing but down. However, a bag labeled simply as containing "down" can have up to 20 percent down fiber (barbs that have become detached from down), waterfowl feather fiber, and waterfowl feathers. Feathers, in particular, lack the resiliency, loftiness, and durability of down. To get some sense of the feather content, feel the bag. A high feather content makes a bag feel stiff, as if it contained straw, when compared with a bag containing better down.

Labels like "northern," "prime," "white," and "gray" lack any legal definition. They mean about as much as the label "new and improved" on a laundry detergent. By law, the label "goose down" must mean that 90 percent of the down is from that species. Goose down tends to loft better than duck down because the larger bird has larger and more lofty down plumules. However, poor goose down lofts less than good duck down. Most down sold today is a mixture. Fill power per ounce indicates quality better than species. Many of the better manufacturers test their own down regularly—another good assurance of quality.

BAG SHAPE AND FIT

After picking the fill, think about overall shape. Rectangular bags are roomier than tapered, form-fitting, mummy bags, so they feel less confining, but they offer much less warmth for their weight. First, you've got the extra shell and filling to carry around. Second, you've got larger pockets of air around you. When you roll over, you tend to expel that warm air through the bag's entrance, then suck cold air back in. Third, the heat loss from a bag is related to its surface area. Rectangular bags have more surface area than mummy bags, which means a higher rate of heat loss. Since your heat output is nearly constant when you're asleep, that means you need a thicker bag if it's rectangular than if it's a mummy. Nearly all winter bags intended for *your* back, not a horse's, are mummies.

Good sleeping bags generally come in different lengths. Choosing the right length is a bit more complicated than just picking one that will accommodate your height.

Unlike some people, I don't generally strip down to my long underwear before sliding into my bag. In fact, I generally wear at least my fleece bibs and a hooded fleece sweater on top of my long johns. That means I want a sleeping bag with enough girth to accommodate that much clothing—and even more in a pinch. I also want enough room to bring a quart water bottle inside (checked carefully beforehand for leaks!). Filling a bottle the night before with melted snow saves time in the morning. I sleep with my inner boots on my feet, leaving the shells outside, so I don't need enough extra length to accommodate my boots. I do put my gaiters into a stuff sack at the bottom of the bag, since I find the zippers freeze solid if they're left outside.

The only way to be certain a bag fits is to shuck your shoes and crawl inside with all the gear you intend to sleep with. Remember that you not only have to sleep in the bag, you may have to live in it for a few days if you get storm-bound on your next traverse of the Patagonian icecap. Decide if it fits with that in mind. A sleeping bag shouldn't feel like a straitjacket.

How much loft you need depends on your metabolism and how willing you are to sleep in lots of clothes. Manufacturer's temperature ratings are useful mostly for comparing bags within one bag maker's line, not for comparisons between manufacturers. I've taken a bag rated to minus-5 degrees and slept in it, passably comfortable, when it was minus-33 degrees. However, I was using a vapor-barrier sleeping bag liner and wearing every scrap of clothing I owned, including four hoods and hats. My friend, sleeping beside me in an identical bag with similar amounts of clothing, shivered half the night even when the temperature was 25 degrees warmer.

The best you can do for your first bag is to take the manufacturer's comfort rating as a basic guideline. If in doubt, go a little on the thick side. When you're tired, damp, and underfed and your bag hasn't seen the sun in a week, you'll be glad you did.

DESIGN DETAILS

Once you've found a sleeping bag with the right shape and size, look closely at the hood design. Well-made bags have hoods that seal snugly around your face. The best bags have both an insulated collar that closes around your neck with its own drawstring, and a second, conventional hood that closes around your face. That system blocks the escape of warm air better than a conventional hood alone. It also lets you cinch down the collar while leaving the main portion of the hood open. That helps prevent the moisture in your breath from penetrating the fabric and condensing in the insulation. In many good down bags, the inside portion of the hood is made of a waterproof-breathable fabric, which also helps keep the hood's down dry.

Besides drawstrings, hoods usually have hook-and-loop tabs to fasten them securely after the zipper is closed. Those tabs should be easy to find in the dark and at least an inch wide for good holding power. I've seen systems so complicated that you needed your headlamp on and both arms out of your bag to fasten the hood properly. Once fastened, of course, you couldn't get your arms back inside the bag without unfastening the hood again. The half-inch-wide tabs found on some bags pop open at a sneeze.

Regardless of hood style, don't cinch down the outer hood with your head entirely inside your bag. Your breath will condense and saturate your insulation. With a down bag, you're likely to start losing loft after a few nights unless you can dry it. With either synthetics or down, you're likely to wake up in the middle of the night with some pretty cold, moist fabric caressing your cheeks. Even with the outer hood cinched down loosely you're likely to get some frost forming on the hood if it's cold enough. To shield my skin from direct contact with that frost, I usually wear a hooded fleece sweater with the hood up. If you find yourself constantly tempted to put your head entirely inside the hood, consider getting a warmer bag.

SLEEPING BAG CARE

Clean bags insulate much better than dirty ones. Dirt can cause down and polyester fibers to clump together, which reduces loft. To clean a bag, hand wash it or use a large-capacity, front-loading washer such as those found at commercial Laundromats. Top-loading, agitator-type machines are far too rough on bags. Down is heavy when wet and agitation tends to rip loose the fragile baffles inside the bag that keep down from shifting and clumping. Fiberfill battings can develop thin spots. Use a mild soap that dissolves easily in the local water, then rinse thoroughly. Soap residues kill loft worse than dirt. Take care that the wash-water temperature doesn't exceed 140 degrees. At least some polyester fibers begin to lose their crimp at that temperature, which leads to loss of loft.

Don't wring out a wet bag. Instead, roll the bag in several towels and gently press out the remaining water. Air dry or tumble dry on air-only setting. You can start the drying process on low heat, but you should finish drying on air-only or outside the dryer. No matter what drying method you use, you'll probably have to do a lot of fluffing to restore a down bag's full loft.

Don't dry-clean any kind of bag. Some manufacturers assert that dry cleaning strips down of its natural oils, rendering it brittle. Whether that's true or not, dry cleaning can leave a residue in the bag if the rinse solvent isn't clean enough. Like a soap residue, that can hurt loft. And fumes from chemical residues can make you think you're sleeping alongside the New Jersey Turnpike instead of deep in the piney woods.

Never store either kind of bag in its stuff sack, particularly in some place hot, like the trunk of your car in the summer. Instead, store your bag in an oversize cotton storage bag. Better yet, hang it in a closet. The idea is to avoid compressing the insulation during storage, which will cause loss of loft.

SHELLS, LINERS, AND SLEEPING PADS

Bags with waterproof-breathable or highly water-resistant outer shells are a blessing on extended trips. Snow caves and igloos can be drippy. Frost forms on tent canopies, then sifts down gently when the wind rattles the tent. Spindrift, fine snow carried by the wind, can eddy through snow-cave entrances and tent doors and vents and fall onto your bag. Waterproof-breathable fabrics keep that moisture out of your insulation. That's particularly important with down bags, but not trivial even with synthetics. An alternative is a waterproof-breathable sleeping bag cover.

It's just as important to keep moisture from entering your bag from the inside. That means using a vapor-barrier liner as I discussed in Chapter 2. On long trips, I start using the vapor barrier as soon as I land on the glacier just to keep my bag dry, even if I don't need the warmth.

Your body weight will completely flatten any sleeping bag insulator. To avoid freezing to death through conduction into the cold ground, you need compression-resistant insulation beneath you.

The standard backpacker's foam pad is made of closed-cell foam that gives very little under body weight. Three-eighth and half-inch thicknesses are standard. A three-eighths-inch closed-cell foam pad provides roughly 1.4 clo of insulation. Your winter-weight sleeping bag with six to eight inches of loft still provides three or four inches of insulation above you even when the bottom half is squashed flat. That means you've got eight to ten clo of insulation above you and one-sixth of that or less below if you're using one three-eighths-inch pad.

Furthermore, your body weight is pressing the pad into contact with cold, highly conductive snow, ice, and frozen ground, while the top surface of your bag is only in contact with air. Obviously, one pad alone doesn't do the job in severe cold. You'll find yourself rolling over constantly, trying to rewarm your cold underside. Solution: Carry two pads. Glue them together at one end if you don't want them to shift around. Just don't glue them together everywhere or you won't be able to roll them neatly.

Air mattresses keep you off the cold ground, but the empty space between the top and bottom of the air mattress is large enough that spontaneous convection currents form, draining away heat.

Air mattresses work better if they have open-cell foam inside, which stops convective heat loss. Therm-A-Rest is the most common brand name. They're luxurious to sleep on in moderate temperatures, but still compress a little too much for deep winter nights, leading to cold spots underneath you. And, like all air mattresses, they have an Achilles heel, as a friend of mine demonstrated by playing mumblety-peg near his mattress at the start of a three-week McKinley expedition. A mistimed throw of his knife neatly skewered his mattress. Lacking a patch kit he was literally flat on a very cold back for the rest of the expedition. The moral, of course, is to bring a patch kit. Then hope the valve doesn't fail, which would cause an equally catastrophic, but probably unrepairable, breakdown.

HOME IN A STUFF SACK: TENTS FOR WINTER CAMPING

At dawn the clouds lifted, but the inhabitants of the high camp at 17,200 feet on Mt. McKinley weren't about to celebrate. With clearing came wind: 60, 70, 80 miles per hour and beyond. At six A.M., National Park Service Ranger Roger Robinson crawled out of his beleaguered tent and dashed for his neighbor's. Inside, guide Nick Parker and an assistant huddled against the tent wall on the windward side, trying to keep the poles from snapping like dry spaghetti noodles.

"We've got to dig a snowcave!" Robinson screamed. Parker nodded. Robinson slipped out of the tent and scuttled crab-like across the snow to check on other people.

Climbers everywhere were struggling with their tents. Now and then a foam pad, a sleeping bag—once even a wallet with five-hundred dollars cash—escaped a numb, mittened hand and vanished into the abyss to the north. Then Robinson saw two fully erect dome tents dragging Parker on his face across the snow. Someone had inadvertently removed the last ice axe holding them down. Parker had lunged for them, caught hold of one with each hand, then discovered too late that not even his full body weight could restrain them. The runaway tents dragged him closer and closer to the drop-off at the edge of camp. At the last minute he simply let go and watched both tents sail into the blue.

When the wind finally died, only one tent out of ten remained erect. Credit for its survival belonged more to the four-foot-high snow walls surrounding it than to the tent itself.

No tent light enough to carry comfortably on your back will stand up forever to drifting snow and high winds. Himalayan climbers sometimes use a shelter called a Whillans Box, but as Everest veteran Todd Bibler said, "That's not a tent—that's a building." A Whillans Box weighs 30 pounds. If the weather really gets extreme, it's time to start thinking about a snow cave.

Even if your tent can withstand the wind, your nerves probably won't. Jack Stephenson, founder of a renegade little company called Stephenson Warmlite Equipment, tells the story of a customer named Larry who took one of Stephenson's extra-rugged, three-person tents to the summit of Mt. Washington in search of a 150-mph gale. Larry had an anemometer that read to 90 mph. The winds blasted the needle off the scale. The summit observatory recorded winds between 120 and 132 mph. Larry couldn't stand up in the wind, much less sleep in the thrashing tent. Although the tent survived, Larry decided afterward that he really wasn't interested in sitting through a 150-mph wind.

Despite all these warnings, I much prefer living in a tent to living in a snow cave whenever weather conditions permit. Digging a cave is hard manual labor that sucks up a lot more energy and time than pitching a tent. Caves can't be dug everywhere, either. The snow may be too shallow or too unconsolidated, or, in the high, glaciated ranges, you may hit blue ice a foot or two below the surface. In good weather, living in a snow cave is like living in a freezer, while tents warm up beautifully when hit by direct sun.

WINTER TENT DESIGNS

The simplest "tent" is nothing more than a waterproof fabric sack, called a bivy sack. Some come with flexible wands that support the fabric around your face. They're big enough to sleep in, but not big enough to cook, dress, or even play solitaire inside. Only mountaineers on extreme routes where the ledges aren't big enough to pitch a tent take bivy sacks.

Tents suitable for winter come in two basic shapes. Dome tents look just like the name implies. Their interlocking pole structure gives them great strength and a minimum amount of unsupported fabric for the wind to attack. All those poles do increase the weight, however. Two-person domes typically range from seven to nine pounds. They have about 35 percent more volume than an old-fashioned A-frame tent of equivalent floor area and height. Domes are free-standing, but must be staked to keep them from blowing away. They're also stronger if the corners are nailed down.

A second popular design for winter tents is the hoop or "Conestoga wagon." This design resembles the traditional A-frame except that the poles are inverted Us instead of inverted Vs. The design's advantage is reduced weight compared to a dome tent (because of fewer poles) and about 58 percent more volume than an A-frame of equal height and floor area. Two-person hoop tents run from three to six pounds. Their disadvantage is that less of the tent fabric is directly supported by the poles. However, well-made hoop tents pitch skin-taut. Tents that don't flap rarely rip from wind load alone. Hoop tents typically only need one or two stakes at each end.

In recent years, yet another variation has debuted: hub tents, in which flexible poles radiate from one or more molded plastic hubs located along the tent's spine. The pole structure gives some hub tents the look of sinister sci-fi insects; one designer named his creation the Preying Mantis. The principal advantage claimed for hub designs is that the poles cannot move in relation to each other where they intersect, since they're connected via a rigid hub. This increases the tent's rigidity and therefore its ability to resist wind and shed snow. Hub designs can also be lighter, since not all poles have to reach to the ground; instead, they can terminate at a hub. In most hub designs, the poles remain attached to the hub at one end with elastic shock cord. Theoretically at least, this can simplify pitching.

Traditional A-frame and single-pole pyramid tents have about vanished from the packs of serious winter campers. Though sturdy, the amount of usable volume per square foot of floor area is small because of the uniformly sloping tent walls. Hoop and dome tents have nearly vertical walls near the floor. Another drawback is that A-frames and pyramids usually require lots of stakes. The large areas of unsupported fabric mean that pyramids, in particular, flap horribly in the wind.

CONDENSATION IN TENTS

Most people think a tent should keep them dry, period. In truth, that task is partly the tent's job, and partly yours. Let's talk about the tent's job first.

It's relatively easy to build a tent that will keep rain and snow out. The tougher task, in many situations, is preventing condensation inside the tent from soaking the occupants.

The air inside a tent is typically humid. Each time you exhale, you add moisture to the air. Evaporation from damp clothing and equipment adds more moisture. The water vapor in any sample of air, if cooled enough, will condense to water droplets. The temperature at which condensation begins is called the dew point. If the tent fabric's temperature is below the dew point, water vapor will condense on it.

The most common tent design keeps rain and snow out with a waterproof, coated fly that is stretched over an uncoated, breathable canopy. In theory, water vapor inside the tent will pass through the uncoated canopy fabric and condense on the fly. Water droplets will run down the fly and drip onto the ground; frost on the fly will be shaken off by tent movement, then fall onto the tent canopy and slide down to the snow.

In practice, water vapor doesn't always pass through the uncoated canopy. In some temperature/humidity combinations, both above and below freezing, the temperature of the canopy can drop below the dew point, which means water vapor condenses right there. I still remember waking up at 17,200 feet on McKinley to find a miniature snowstorm raging inside the tent. Moisture from three deep-breathing bodies had condensed to frost on the canopy. With each gust of wind, frost feathers broke loose from the canopy and sifted down over everything. Each morning we would pile all our gear in one corner, scrape down the walls, sweep the floor, and shovel the sweepings out the door. Standard double-wall tent design by itself doesn't always solve the condensation problem.

A second approach to the condensation problem is to build a single-wall tent from a waterproof/breathable fabric. Such tents are very light and easy to pitch. Gore-Tex, one obvious choice for such a tent, has not been available for tent use under that name since 1986 because it could not meet fire-resistance standards in some states. However, Todd Bibler found a way to make a tent fabric using essentially the same process that he calls ToddTex. His tents, now available through Black Diamond Equipment, are very expensive but work very well. I've been using mine, winter and summer, for five years and have found condensation to be well controlled.

At first glance, the third approach to condensation control looks like it would generate the worst condensation. In reality, it may well cause the least. Since 1957, Stephenson Warmlite Equipment has been making double-walled tents using coated fabrics for both the fly and the canopy. The coating on the canopy prevents warm, moist air from reaching the cold fly, so the fly stays drier. The canopy coating also helps keep warm air in the tent, which keeps the canopy warmer and thus more often above the dew point. To keep the canopy warmer still, Stephenson tents use an aluminized ripstop to reduce radiant heat loss. I've used tents with this design for a total of eighty-five days in the Alaska Range. Compared to standard design, condensation was always minimal.

THE NEED FOR VENTILATION

None of these three approaches can solve the condensation problem entirely on its own. The ventilation system is just as important. The key to successful ventilation is the chimney effect. Warm air rises. To let it escape, there must be a vent near the tent peak. Air can't flow both in and out of one vent at the same time, so there must be another vent where cold air enters to replace the warm. Logically, that vent should be near the floor.

Tents with vents at only one level, be it high or low, do not ventilate nearly as well as tents with both high and low vents. Vents should be covered with very fine no-see-um netting, which effectively stops most wind-driven snow. Zippered covers over the vents prevent snow from entering in really nasty conditions. Be sure you don't seal up your tent completely; even in a blizzard, you should always keep a vent open on the leeward side.

DESIGN DETAILS

The best tents today come with factory-sealed seams. If they aren't factory-sealed, you should do it yourself. Floor seams, in particular, can be chronic leak points. Look for a "bathtub floor," in which the floor/sidewall seams are raised above the ground.

Doors can be another leak point. Tunnel entrances prevent snow and rain from entering when you're exiting, but they also turn your exit into an awkward reenactment of the birth experience. Zippered entrances set into a sloping surface can be a problem if snow builds up on the tent wall. Opening the door tends to allow snow to pour in. Doors that flip out sideways toss any snow buildup away from the interior. Doors that fold down when opened drop snow buildup right into the tent unless you knock the snow off carefully beforehand.

Some tents come with a choice of fiberglass or aluminum poles. While recent improvements in fiberglass have increased its strength, it's still inherently weaker and heavier than the best aluminum. It's also cheaper.

WINTER CAMPING 101

Taking care opening the tent door is just one of the ways you can do your part to prevent your dry, snug tent from becoming a swimming pool. You should also minimize the amount of moisture you bring inside. Bringing clothing soaked with rain or sweat inside to dry invites condensation. Shed your rain gear before getting into the tent, then turn the garments inside out so the moisture won't evaporate off them. If the tent walls do get wet, wipe them down with a sponge. If they get frosty, pile your gear in a corner and scrape them off. Then use the small whisk broom you remembered to bring to sweep up the frost as well as any snow that's blown in and toss it out the door.

Although many people do it, cooking inside a tent is a dangerous practice that should be avoided. Most tents are fire-resistant, meaning they won't continue to burn after the ignition source is put out. But they will certainly burn if you've got a flaming pool of gasoline on your tent floor! Even if you're careful to prevent fire, the invisible, odorless carbon monoxide produced by all stoves can kill you. Two very experienced mountaineers died on McKinley in 1986 from carbon monoxide poisoning caused by cooking inside a sealed tent. Tired from a hard day, they apparently fell asleep while the stove was running and never woke up.

In the tent failures I've seen, the poles snapped first, then the jagged ends tore the fabric. Poles stressed over time, especially if the protective anodizing has worn off, can fail suddenly even without additional loading through a phenomenon called stress-corrosion cracking. This is why tent makers recommend you keep your poles clean. Dirty poles corrode faster. A short length of copper tubing with an inside diameter slightly larger than the outside diameter of the pole can be used to splice a break.

Even the best poles eventually fatigue after enough flexing in punishing winds. Eventually, they will break, sometimes under a lower load than they withstood earlier. If your poles have taken a

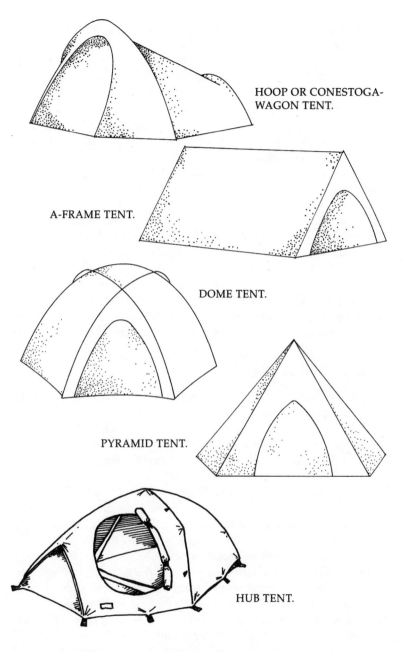

HOOP OR CONESTOGA-WAGON TENT.

A-FRAME TENT.

DOME TENT.

PYRAMID TENT.

HUB TENT.

TENT DESIGNS.

beating in the past, it's a good idea to replace them before embarking on another major expedition.

Tent poles are usually held together with elastic shock cord. In severe cold, the shock cord can lose its elasticity. That's not a problem taking the tent down. However, reassembling the poles can be difficult because the stretched-out shock cord won't contract and fit back inside the poles. The solution is to rapidly and repeatedly stretch and release the cord. That warms it enough to regain its elasticity and slip back inside the pole.

Conventional tent stakes are worthless in deep snow. To anchor your tent in the winter, tie long, stout cords to the tent-stake loops along the perimeter of the tent floor. Then tie those cords to nearby trees or to skis or snowshoes inserted tail-first into the snow. If you're going to be needing those items before you take the tent down, try tying the anchor cords to the drawstring of a stuff sack. Fill the stuff sack with snow, dig a hole deep enough to accommodate the stuff sack with a foot of room to spare, drop in the filled stuff sack, and pack snow on top. Once the snow has had a chance to set, you'll be surprised at how strong such an anchor can be. A shovel is normally required to dig the stuff sack back out.

BUYING A TENT

Before buying a tent, if possible, pitch it first. A good winter tent should pitch as taut as a sail in a stiff breeze. Canopy strength comes not so much from heavy materials as a design that distributes the load evenly and has reinforcements at the stress points. You shouldn't need bare hands to pitch it, though a surprising number of otherwise good tents demand that kind of dexterity. Sometimes it's possible to add a loop of webbing to the tent body to make it easier to grasp with gloved hands. If the pole diameter is large enough, you can drill a hole through the end and tie a loop of string through it to give you something to grab.

The typical sporting goods store rarely carries tents good enough to take on a serious winter camping trip. High-quality winter tents are too expensive to appeal to such a store's typical customer. The same is true of most of the other gear I've been talking about. In general, you'll find the best gear in specialty mountaineering, backpacking, and cross-country skiing shops. Try to find a well-stocked shop so the salesperson sells you what you need, not what he or she happens to have on hand.

If you can't find a specialty shop nearby, consider mail order from one of the big, reputable mail-order houses like EMS or REI. Or shop online. You'll find some phone numbers and Web sites in the appendix to get you started.

WHITE PALACES: HOW TO BUILD SNOW CAVES AND IGLOOS

Our fifth day on the south face of Mt. Hunter dawned stormy. Anxious about our dwindling food, we started climbing again nonetheless. Twelve hours later, with the snow still falling in blankets and darkness closing in, we began searching for a bivy site. Every possibility within view would have required hours of chopping to make it level. We got out our headlamps and kept climbing.

About ten P.M. I saw through the mist and snow that Peter had stopped. As I joined him he said, "We might get tent platforms here!" I thrust an ice axe deep into the yielding snow and realized we might get something better: a snow cave.

Two hours later, wet and exhausted, we crawled into a snug, quiet, storm-proof heaven. The cave seemed all the more luxurious in contrast to the marginal shelter of the hooped bivy sacks we'd used during the previous four nights. The stove and our body heat soon raised the temperature to near freezing. We broke into a ragged chorus of "Shelter from the Storm" and laughed for the first time in hours. We dug caves every night for the next five.

SNOW CAVES

A snow cave is the easiest snow shelter to build. That cave on Hunter was my first one. To build a simple cave, just find a hillside

CROSS-SECTION OF A SNOW CAVE.

with five or six feet of snow on it and start digging. Keep the entrance small, and enlarge as you get deeper. To build a really snug cave, dig straight into the hillside, then up, and then begin expanding. That places the entrance lower than the floor of the cave, which helps trap warm air in the cave and keep out spindrift.

You can dig a cave on flat ground, but it means moving more snow because you have to dig down first. Hillsides also form better cave sites because you can throw the snow straight out the entrance, then shovel it down the slope rather than lifting each shovelful to the surface. Poke an ice axe or ski pole through the roof for ventilation, then close the entrance once you're inside with packs or a large block of snow.

If the snow is wet, so that it sticks together well, you can ease the task of caving on flat ground by making a pile of snow several feet high and a couple of feet larger in diameter than the finished shelter you want. Pack it down well, then let it sit for twenty minutes. Shoveling snow into a pile breaks flakes into smaller particles that quickly begin to bond together if given a few minutes. When the snow has set, dig down to the side of the pile, tunnel underneath, then hollow out the pile to form a hybrid snow cave/igloo.

Be sure to avoid potential avalanche paths when siting a snow shelter. Several years ago twenty members of the Colorado Mountain Club were digging practice snow caves beneath a small hill, well below timberline. A slab avalanche over four feet thick buried two of them. Only one survived. Any open, treeless slope lying at an angle between 30 and 45 degrees, even if it's only a hundred feet high, should be considered dangerous unless you know enough about avalanches to prove otherwise.

Ideally, the cave entrance should face at right angles to the prevailing wind. If it faces directly into the wind, of course, snow blows in. Paradoxically, the same thing can happen if the entrance faces directly away from the wind and is sited just below a ridgecrest. We learned that the unpleasant way on Mt. Hunter. When we woke up after our eighth night, two inches of snow covered our sleeping bags and all our gear.

Only later did I learn why. Ridges accelerate wind by compressing a large volume of air and forcing it through a smaller space, the region just above the ridgecrest. Similarly, a broad river may flow very slowly, but if forced into a narrow canyon, it will accelerate. When the river escapes the canyon, it slows once more. Eddies, places where the river actually flows upstream, may form where the river widens abruptly. In the same way, wind decelerates just after it passes over a ridgecrest and may double back on itself in a vortex. That vortex can carry snow into your cave.

To dig a cave effectively, you'll need a shovel. Plastic-bladed shovels are very light, and work just fine for digging a cave in soft snow, or for excavating a tent buried by drifting snow. However, they simply bounce off the snow when used to dig for an avalanche victim. Avalanche debris usually sets up rock-hard. Everyone traveling in avalanche country should carry an avalanche beacon to help find a buried victim and an aluminum-bladed shovel to dig the victim out. Avalanche safety and rescue is a big topic. Dozens of books have been written on the topic. See a specialty outdoor-equipment retailer or an online bookstore like Amazon.com for the latest offerings.

Be sure to keep your cave well-ventilated. Body and stove heat can glaze the cave's interior with ice, effectively sealing it. Poke an ice axe or ski pole shaft through the roof if drifting snow threatens to block the entrance. Work the axe or ski pole in circles until you have a hole three inches in diameter. It's a good idea to bring one shovel inside, so you can dig yourself out more easily if the entrance does get buried.

Digging a cave takes a lot of wet, hard work. Don all your shell gear and your overmitts, pull up your hood and seal your cuffs before diving into the hole. Creating a decent-size two-person cave requires moving about 150 cubic feet of snow. Be prepared to spend at least an hour in soft snow, two or three in hard snow. In really hard snow, you may need to use an ice ax. If you hit genuine ice near the surface, try another site. You can only remove about one cubic inch of hard ice with one blow of an ice axe. To remove one cubic foot takes about 1,700 blows. Your aching shoulders will soon convince you to move elsewhere.

IGLOOS

Fortunately, if the snow is hard enough to make snow-caving difficult (and if you have a snow saw), you can build alternative shelters out of snow blocks. Snow saws are simply coarse-toothed saws, usually one and a half to two feet long. Pruning saws work quite well, although the sharp teeth tend to chew up your pack. Snow saws specifically designed for the task usually have blunter teeth.

To build the simplest snow-block shelter, dig a trench three feet wide and six or seven feet long. Then place big snow blocks on edge on either side and lean them up against each other like an A-frame tent. Cutting your snow blocks from a hole that will become your trench saves energy. These shelters usually accommodate only one person because blocks big enough to span a two-person trench often won't hold together.

The first-class snow-block shelter is the igloo. The procedure for building one may sound complicated, but it's actually easier than it looks. Three friends and I completed our first igloo on our first try at our basecamp below Mt. Huntington. We neglected only one problem: the potency of the sun in the Alaska Range in July. When clear skies finally returned after a week of storm, the igloo promptly collapsed.

Good snow for blocks should be firm enough that your boot heel barely dents it as you walk. Start by cutting a group of blocks of identical size, each roughly two feet long, 18 inches high, and six inches thick. Arrange them in a circle, leaning inward slightly. As

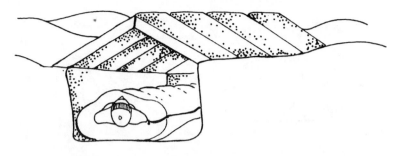

THIS TYPE OF SNOW SHELTER CONSISTS OF A TRENCH COVERED
WITH SNOW BLOCKS LEANING AGAINST ONE ANOTHER.

you place each block, bevel the vertical side so it fits flush against its
neighbor. When you have one row complete, take your snow saw
and turn your block wall into a circular ramp that starts at ground
level and curves around to one block height after a full circle. The
beginning and end of the ramp will be adjacent to each other.

Now begin laying on blocks again, starting at the ramp's
thinnest point. You will be building a rising spiral of blocks. Each
new block is supported both by the block beneath and by its neighbor to one side. It's the support of the block to one side that allows
you to lean each row of blocks in a little farther. One member of
your group should stay inside to support and trim each block while
the next is laid in place. The final block, the keystone, is trimmed to
be wedge-shaped and then slipped carefully into a matching hole.
Chink the holes with soft snow or bits of broken blocks, saw out a
door, and you've got a sturdy home. If you want to do it fancy, cut
your blocks from a trench, then lay your first circle of blocks so the
end of the trench is three feet inside the igloo. The trench then
becomes the entrance. Since it's lower than the igloo floor, the igloo
stays a bit warmer, just like in a snowcave. If you want to keep your
igloo tidy but don't want to go outside to relieve yourself in the
middle of the night, bring in an extra snow block to use as a chamber pot, then dispose of it outside in the morning.

SNOW WALLS

If you enjoy the light admitted by a tent, and its warmth when
the sun shines, but need the shelter of an igloo, consider using snow

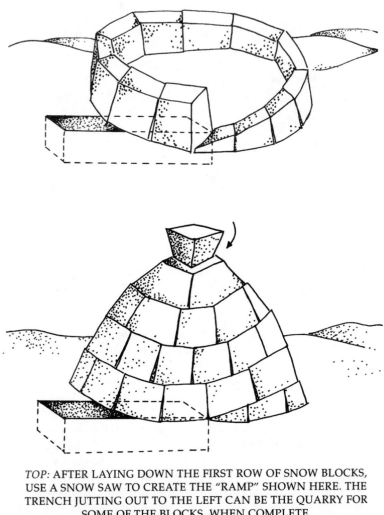

TOP: AFTER LAYING DOWN THE FIRST ROW OF SNOW BLOCKS, USE A SNOW SAW TO CREATE THE "RAMP" SHOWN HERE. THE TRENCH JUTTING OUT TO THE LEFT CAN BE THE QUARRY FOR SOME OF THE BLOCKS. WHEN COMPLETE, THE TRENCH SERVES AS THE ENTRANCEWAY.
BOTTOM: TO COMPLETE THE IGLOO, SHAPE A CAPSTONE BLOCK TO FIT AND SET IT GENTLY INTO PLACE.

to deflect wind from your tent. The simplest but least effective system is to dig a huge hole and pitch your tent inside. Although the walls of the hole effectively stop wind, wind-carried snow will quickly bury your tent. Wind even in the absence of precipitation can move a tremendous amount of snow. Drifts can deepen at the rate of one and a half feet per hour. However, 90 percent of that wind-carried snow is confined to the first 18 inches above the surface.

To stop drifting snow from burying you immediately, build a block wall around your pit at least 18 inches high, preferably higher. It saves work to take the blocks from the area that will become the pit. You'll still get some snow piling up on your tent in high winds because the wind will decelerate slightly as it passes over the top of the wall, just as it does when passing over a ridge crest. Slower winds hold less snow, which means some snow drops out of the gale and fills in the gap between the wall and the tent.

Block walls must be substantial to withstand severe winds. Wind's first weapon is erosion. Wind whistling through the chinks in a wall gradually wears away the corners of each block. Eventually you have a stack of cannonballs instead of bricks, which can collapse with the next gust. I've seen tent poles break when struck by falling walls. You can strengthen both snow walls and igloos by chinking the cracks and by pouring water over the junctions between blocks to freeze them together.

Really vicious winds can simply knock walls down. In 1984 I built a wall around my tent at 17,200 feet on McKinley using blocks two feet long and a foot square. Moving each block made me gasp. After the wind knocked the wall down twice, I finally rebuilt it using the blocks so that their long axis was perpendicular to the wall. That made the wall two feet thick. At last I had a "Maginot Line" that could withstand the wind's punishment. It took so much work to build that I was joking about auctioning it off when I left. But I slept soundly once it was done, which made it worth every ounce of energy.

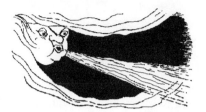

CARE OF THE HUMAN ANIMAL: PREVENTION, RECOGNITION, AND TREATMENT OF HYPOTHERMIA AND FROSTBITE

I knew that moving our camp from 14,300 feet to 17,200 feet on McKinley would stress my clients severely. But I didn't know how close one client—Marilyn—would come to serious trouble.

The day began with a 2,000-foot climb up an ever-steepening snow wall. Everyone, particularly Marilyn, was tired at the top, and we still had to gain 1,000 feet of elevation up an exposed ridge. The wind began picking up.

We pulled into camp about five P.M. The increasing wind and dropping temperatures forced everyone, including Marilyn, to rummage through their packs for more warm clothes. We began digging a giant snow cave in case McKinley's weather machine really ran amok.

Marilyn chipped in for a while, then, without my noticing it, slipped into the tent we had erected as temporary shelter for people while they added extra clothing. Half an hour later, a client emerged from the tent after pulling on another layer and said to me, "Marilyn seems to be getting very cold. Maybe you should check on her."

I crawled into the tent immediately and called her name. She only moaned in reply and suddenly I got worried. Fortunately, two of my clients had bags that zipped together. I borrowed those and zipped them into one giant bag. Then an assistant and I shed some of our outer layers, removed some of Marilyn's outer layers, put her in the double sleeping bag, and crawled in with her. We wanted our warmth to reach her without obstruction by lots of insulation, which keeps heat out as effectively as it keeps heat in. Meanwhile, another assistant managed to get a stove going outside in the wind. Soon he brought in a bottle of piping hot water and, shortly thereafter, another. We laid them on Marilyn's stomach.

To my relief, she began to warm up within an hour. When she was fully conscious, we gave her sweet drinks, then soup, then solid food. Soon she was able to move into her own sleeping bag. Although bouts of shivering continued to attack her occasionally for several more hours, the danger was clearly over.

For a while, Marilyn had been seriously hypothermic. Had the dangerous drop in her core body temperature continued untreated, it could have been fatal. Below a core temperature of about 94 degrees, people can become incapable of rewarming themselves no matter how much insulation is added. Some form of external heat must be provided.

Almost every possible factor had combined to predispose Marilyn to hypothermia. She hadn't been eating enough for days, in part because altitude and exertion had made her stomach queasy. Not eating enough meant she had little fuel to burn to generate warmth. Her low blood sugar, a consequence of eating too little, decreased her ability to shiver, one of the body's main mechanisms for generating heat. She also hadn't been drinking enough and was almost certainly dehydrated. Dehydration aggravates the effects of hypothermia.

Marilyn's inadequate food intake had slimmed her already trim build still further. Thin people have less insulating fat, so they cool faster. She also had the disadvantage of being fairly short. Small people have a greater surface area in proportion to their volume than big people, which means faster heat loss. Infants are the most susceptible of all in this regard, particularly because they can't shiver effectively.

Marilyn was also not very fit, which meant the hard work of climbing to 17,200 feet exhausted her even more than the rest of us. Exhaustion also reduced her ability to shiver. The amount of oxygen consumed by an active, mildly hypothermic individual is much larger than the amount consumed by the same person when warm. That oxygen consumption reflects the greater energy cost of working with cold muscles. Marilyn probably started to get chilled even before she reached camp. Had she stayed warm during the day, she would probably have arrived less exhausted. Hypothermia and exhaustion link arms, each goading the other on.

The final contributing factor to Marilyn's hypothermia was the high altitude. The air's lower oxygen content probably caused her to become somewhat hypoxic, a condition in which insufficient oxygen reaches the body's tissues. Hypoxia also decreases shivering.

Simply being a woman probably didn't affect her chances of hypothermia. Although women, on average, are smaller than men and have a slightly lower basal metabolism (amount of heat produced at rest), their higher level of insulating body fat evens the score. Women in cold-water immersion tests cool at very nearly the same rate as men. Other factors besides sex play a larger role in who is most susceptible.

Fortunately, Marilyn didn't make the mistake of drinking alcohol or taking tranquilizers or sleeping pills. These drugs decrease shivering and help predispose a person to hypothermia. She also wasn't injured. Injuries, by causing shock, can make victims more susceptible to rapid cooling.

Given everything Marilyn had working against her, I didn't have much hope she'd make the summit. Although reaching the top from 17,200 feet takes only a day, the cold, wind, and even higher altitude conspire to make that day even more grueling than the day getting to 17,200 feet. We hunkered down in our tents and began waiting for the weather to clear.

BODY MAINTENANCE MADE SIMPLE

So far in this book, I've talked mostly about using gear intelligently to slow the rate of heat loss from your body. Now it's time to talk about the other side of the equation: how your body generates heat and what you can do to help it.

Heat generation must balance heat loss or you will soon be either sweating or shivering. Your body generates heat by breaking down food molecules. When you're inactive, nearly all the energy derived from the metabolism of food eventually appears as heat. When you're active, roughly 20 percent of the chemical energy in food is used to move the working muscles. The rest becomes heat.

A few animals, such as rats, can acclimatize to cold by learning to burn food faster, thereby generating more heat, without constant shivering and without working the large muscles. Studies of men winterizing in Antarctica, however, have found only debatable evidence that people raised in temperate climates can achieve an equivalent kind of cold acclimatization, even given several months.

There is some evidence that cold-acclimatized Antarctic residents experience a more rapid and severe vasoconstriction when exposed to cold than they did before going to Antarctica, but this is a means of restricting heat loss, not increasing heat production. Intense vasoconstriction predisposes your hands and feet to frostbite, besides being quite uncomfortable, so it cannot be an adequate defense against the cold.

Hands, by contrast, acclimatize to cold quite well. Even if you're not used to cold, you will experience something called "cold-induced vasodilatation" when your hands are chilled. Every seven to 15 minutes, the vasoconstriction in your hands will be replaced briefly by vasodilatation. This "hunting reaction" causes your hands to feel warmer and less stiff. Expose your hands to cold long enough and often enough, and the periods of vasodilatation will become more frequent, more intense, and longer-lived.

A few groups of people have developed an amazing tolerance for cold. Charles Darwin reported seeing native women in Tierra del Fuego nursing their babies while snow fell on their bare breasts, apparently oblivious to the cold. Australian aborigines can remain asleep when their core temperature begins to drop, unlike non-aborigines, who almost invariably wake up shivering miserably. No one fully understands the mechanisms of this cold adaptation, despite a good deal of research. For most people, cold acclimatization is something to fantasize about as we reach for another heavy sweater. Without clothing, most people are only comfortable when the temperature exceeds 80 degrees.

Unless you're an aborigine or Tierra del Fuegan, shivering is the only mechanism by which you can consistently generate more heat when you're inactive. Intense shivering increases heat production to five times the resting rate. Strenuous exercise, however, increases it even more, and is much more useful if you use that energy to build an igloo or hike like a runaway locomotive to escape a cold situation you can't deal with. Even the most vigorous exercise, however, cannot compensate for heat lost in severe cold unless you have adequate clothing.

EATING RIGHT

As you can see, you can't do much short of shivering or performing jumping jacks to increase your body's heat production. But you can do a lot to keep heat production from falling. To start with, that means eating enough food.

The amount of food required when you're inactive, whether in the cold or not, is pretty constant. That's because our basal metabolic rate doesn't rise significantly in cold weather. However, movement in the cold does cost more energy than moving in a warm climate, primarily because you're working against the resistance of all that heavy clothing. You're also constantly picking up heavy boots and frequently picking up skis or snowshoes as well. In addition, you're fighting the resistance of the snow. Two studies in Antarctica concluded that outdoor work cost twice as much energy there as it would have in a temperate climate.

Eating a meal increases metabolism by about ten percent for the next four to six hours. You should eat at least that often, and many experienced winter travelers stop every two hours or so. Never let yourself get ravenous. Munching frequently has the added advantage that your nibble-stops need not be long. That helps prevent the chilling that happens so easily if you stop for a long time and neglect to add clothing. A friend calls this the "shark theory of staying warm." Most sharks must swim constantly to keep water flowing through their gills, which is what enables them to breathe. In a similar way, humans in severe cold stay warm most easily by moving nearly constantly when they're not in their sleeping bags.

Carbohydrates and protein give about 110 calories per ounce, fats about 250. It's tempting to increase the fat content of your diet if you're concerned about the total number of calories you can carry on your back, but a fatty diet quickly becomes unpalatable. It's also bad for your health over the long term. Carbohydrates digest faster than fats, so if you need some energy quickly, go for them. On a long trip, you'll need to balance all three major kinds of food to get adequate amounts of vitamins and minerals as well as calories.

THE NEED FOR WATER

Drinking inadequate amounts of water doesn't directly cause hypothermia, but it greatly aggravates its effects. To understand that, you need to understand how hypothermia alone affects the circulatory system.

Cold acts directly to increase blood's viscosity. Cold also causes some of the blood's water content to leave the circulatory system and become trapped in the body's other tissues, which increases viscosity further. Finally, cold causes the spleen to contract, which increases the number of red blood cells in circulation, again increasing viscosity.

Cold also causes the overall volume of blood to drop through a phenomenon called "cold diuresis." When you start to get cold, the blood vessels near the skin constrict to save precious heat. All that blood is shunted to the core, where the kidneys perceive it as surplus. The kidneys then extract the water, which passes out as urine.

The result of all these different effects of cold on circulation is a low volume of thick, hard-to-pump blood being pushed around by a heart that itself becomes weaker as its temperature drops. Since blood carries oxygen, that means the body's cells receive less oxygen. Oxygen is critical to their normal functioning.

Dehydration compounds hypothermia's dangerous effects on circulation by further reducing blood volume. The blood thickens still more, circulates more slowly, and provides even less oxygen to the oxygen-starved cells.

Fluid losses go way up in the cold even if you avoid cold diuresis by staying warm. Cold air holds little water vapor compared to warm air, even when the cold air's relative humidity is 100 percent. Cold air is always dry.

When you inhale that dry air, you warm it through contact with your nose, mouth, throat, and lungs. The warmed air absorbs moisture from the moist linings of your respiratory system. The result is that fluid losses from your lungs go up. Given the same level of activity, you always need to drink more in the cold than you do at moderate temperatures.

High fluid losses, combined with the serious consequences of failing to drink enough, mean you must drink a lot to stay healthy in the cold. Unfortunately, your body won't tell you accurately how much you need to drink. It will tell you when you're thirsty, but simply putting something in your mouth decreases the sensation of thirst for about fifteen minutes. People tend to drink a cup when they need a couple of quarts. The easiest way to tell if you're drinking enough is to monitor the color of your urine. Passing large quantities of clear urine (about one and a half quarts every twenty-four hours, if you care to measure) is a good sign you're drinking enough. A volume of less than half a quart signals that you're getting dehydrated.

To pass a quart and a half of urine, you may need to drink anywhere from half a gallon to a gallon and a half of water every day, depending on the degree of cold, your level of exertion, and, most important, your altitude. Mountaineers at high altitude may need as much as a gallon a day just to humidify the air they breathe, according to James Wilkerson, co-author of *Hypothermia, Frostbite, and Other Cold Injuries*. Sweat, urine output, and insensible perspiration (the fluid lost through your skin that is not produced by sweat glands) can easily account for another two quarts.

High altitude also affects susceptibility to hypothermia in other ways. Water evaporating from lung and throat linings extracts heat just like it does when it evaporates from your skin. Panting in the thin air increases heat loss as well as fluid loss. Loss of appetite and insensitivity to thirst also commonly afflict people at altitude.

To defend yourself when you go high, you must consciously force yourself to eat and drink enough. If your dipstick reads low, you don't ask your car whether it's thirsty before giving it a quart of oil. In the same way, you don't ask your body whether it's thirsty or hungry when you pull into a high-altitude camp. You just start drinking and munching.

STOVES

Backcountry travelers in winter need a lot of water, yet most liquid sources are frozen solid. That makes a reliable stove to melt water from snow a crucial piece of cold-weather equipment. Backpacking stoves are available that burn white gas (more properly called naptha), kerosene, and butane. In general, white-gas stoves that come with a pump for increasing the amount of vaporized gasoline forced through the nozzle provide the highest heat output in the cold. They can be temperamental, however, so look for a model that can be stripped down, cleaned, and repaired in the field with simple tools and spare parts.

Butane stoves, because they're simpler, are often more reliable. Current models actually burn a mixture of butane and propane, which works better than pure butane in cold weather. High altitude actually improves a butane stove's performance because the lower atmospheric pressure means a lower boiling point for butane, just as it does for water. More butane vaporizes per minute, and so the stove burns hotter. In most wintertime situations, however, you'll be better served by a white-gas stove.

For a complete treatise on backpacking stoves, see *The Outward Bound Backpacker's Handbook*, also published by The Lyons Press.

HYPOTHERMIA

Armed with knowledge, experience, and the right equipment, you need not fear hypothermia. But the odds are decent that some day a member of your group, or someone you meet in the backcountry, will become hypothermic. Here's how to recognize the problem and correct it.

For the purpose of discussion, let's divide hypothermia into two types, mild and profound, although the progression of symptoms isn't broken into sharply defined stages. Mild hypothermia begins with cold toes and fingers and a general sensation of feeling chilly. Victims are usually shivering, though that may not be apparent when they're moving. People who are shivering clearly need to get their heat equations back in balance.

Mild hypothermia causes other problems, too. As muscles cool, they become progressively stiffer, weaker, and less coordinated. Clumsiness usually strikes hands first. More severely hypothermic victims frequently have trouble walking on rough terrain. Their speech may become slurred. They usually lose interest in whatever goal they were originally pursuing and become interested only in getting warm.

In profound hypothermia, muscular deterioration becomes more pronounced, until victims may no longer be able to stand. Shivering usually stops at a core temperature of 90 to 92, although individuals vary widely in this. Apathy takes over completely. Profoundly hypothermic people frequently fail to do all they can to keep themselves from getting colder. They leave jacket zippers unzipped, or fail to get all the way into their sleeping bag, or forget to put on hats and gloves.

An even more serious confusion follows. Victims of profound hypothermia sometimes fling off their clothes. As cooling continues, victims become comatose. Heart and respiration rates slow and may become practically imperceptible. Eventually, heart failure causes death.

Treatment for mild hypothermia is simple: Rewarm the victim

immediately by any convenient means! First, stop the heat loss. If the victim has fallen into a lake or stream, take off the wet clothing and put on dry. If you don't have dry clothing, at least wring out the wet clothing thoroughly, then put it back on. Put something waterproof and not breathable on top: raingear, a plastic groundsheet, or a large plastic garbage bag with holes for the head and arms. If the victim is dry, add more clothing, or get him or her into a sleeping bag.

People with mild hypothermia will eventually rewarm by themselves if they put on lots of dry insulation. To speed the process, add heat. Build a fire or place hot water bottles along the sides of the chest and where the thighs meet the torso. Better yet, get a warm person into the same sleeping bag with the cold one. Zip two bags together if there isn't room inside one.

Hot liquids make a victim feel better and combat dehydration, although they have less actual warming effect on the core than you might think. A pint of hot liquid in the stomach of a 150-pound man provides enough heat to raise the man's temperature by less than half a degree. The feeling of warmth comes because hot liquid flowing down the throat warms the blood flowing to the brain. The brain, thinking the body is too warm, responds by dilating blood vessels in the skin. That makes the victim feel better.

Alcohol also causes vasodilatation, but its other effects are harmful. Alcohol decreases shivering, acts as a diuretic, accelerating dehydration, and impairs judgment. Alcohol shouldn't be given to any hypothermia victim. Shivering can stop if skin temperature goes up, but the core remains cool, so don't leave the fire or shed clothing too soon.

Profound hypothermia is a truly life-threatening emergency. Death can occur through heart failure even after rewarming begins through a complex phenomenon called rewarming shock. Cold has so weakened the heart in profoundly hypothermic victims that simply handling them roughly can cause ventricular fibrillation, in which the heart muscle fibers begin contracting randomly rather than in synch. Death follows within minutes. Victims should not try to help themselves. Literally any movement can cause sudden death.

If you can prevent a victim from cooling any further and a professional rescue team can be summoned within a few hours, your best option is turning the rescue over to them. If that's not possible, very gentle, slow rewarming of the torso only, with absolutely no rough handling, may save a life.

FROSTBITE

Frostbite is the other major danger that cold poses for winter travelers. The same care of your body that will help prevent hypothermia goes a long ways toward preventing frostbite. Keep your core temperature up, and your extremities will stay a lot warmer. That means eating and drinking enough as well as wearing appropriate clothing.

Wind chills bare skin much faster than calm air at the same temperature. Beware of removing your gloves in high wind. Dehydration contributes to frostbite because the drop in blood volume causes the blood to thicken, as I explained earlier. Viscous blood flows more slowly, so it cools further before reaching your extremities, providing less warmth. High altitude also increases the risk of frostbite because altitude decreases cold-induced vasodilatation, even after acclimatization to the thin air.

Tight boots and gloves constrict circulation and greatly increase the risk of frostbite. Stuffing too many socks or liner gloves into your boots or mitten shells, or lacing your bootlaces or crampon straps too tightly, has the same effect. Avoid nicotine, which is a vasoconstrictor.

Sometimes just getting your weight off your feet by sitting down for a few minutes can help numb toes rewarm. Another strategy is to stand on one leg and swing your foot back and forth vigorously to drive more warm blood into your toes. This approach can work with cold fingers as well. If your toes stay painfully cold, stop, remove your boots, and inspect them. If necessary, rewarm them with your own hands or by placing them on some tolerant companion's stomach. If you wear warm booties around camp, try to put on your cold boots as the last step before hoisting your pack and heading up the trail. Vigorous exercise will help send warm blood to your feet.

Don't handle metal objects with bare hands. Metal conducts heat more than a thousand times faster than air. On a nice windless, zero-degree day, you may be able to leave your gloves off for several minutes without great discomfort. Grab the metal head of your ice axe, however, and you can have a nasty case of frostbite within seconds.

Extremely cold liquids are equally dangerous because contact between the cold liquid and your skin is so intimate and evaporation is so fast. Gasoline, kerosene, and alcohol all freeze at a much lower temperature than water. Spilling very cold gasoline or kerosene on your skin will cause serious injury. If you leave a bottle of high-proof booze outside your tent on a cold night, then take a swig in the morning, you can freeze the inside of your mouth.

Frostbite's first warning is usually pain, although not for all people. Numbness follows, though again not for everyone. Once the pain stops, it's tempting to think the problem has vanished. Unfortunately, it may only be getting worse. I had no inkling my fingers were becoming frostbitten on Mt. Hunter until I removed my gloves to tighten a crampon strap.

Frostbitten skin usually appears white and hard. If a large area, such as an entire hand or foot, is frozen, the skin may appear purplish because the blood flowing sluggishly in the vessels has clotted. That kind of discoloration usually means much or all of the frostbitten part will be lost.

Frostbite damages tissue in two ways. First, ice crystals form between the cells. These ice crystals extract water from the cells as they grow, damaging the cells physically and chemically. Ice crystals can form within cells, but only if freezing occurs much faster than is normal in frostbite injuries.

More damaging to the tissue than ice crystal formation is the obstruction of the tissue's blood supply. As I mentioned earlier, cold affects the cells lining the capillaries in such a way that they allow the water portion of the blood to leak out into the tissues. The blood that does continue to flow thickens and eventually clots. No oxygen reaches the tissues, leading to permanent damage.

The best treatment for frostbite is rapid rewarming in a water bath between 100 and 108 degrees. In no case should the water temperature exceed 112 degrees. That means it should not feel hot to an uninjured hand. To keep the pot or tub warm, remove the injured limb and add hot water. Stir thoroughly, check the temperature, then put the limb back in. Never use an open flame under the pot to keep it warm. The injured area, while still numb, could come in contact with the bottom of the pot and be severely burned without the victim's knowledge.

Continue thawing for twenty to forty minutes, or until the frozen part flushes pink. Taking one or two aspirin while the part is still frozen and every six hours thereafter may help increase circulation through aspirin's anticlotting properties.

Slow thawing at a lower temperature usually leads to greater tissue loss. Thawing at higher temperatures, such as in front of a fire or over the exhaust of a snowmobile, is a sure prescription for disastrous loss of flesh. The victim cannot feel the heat, which often means that a burn is added on top of the frostbite.

Once thawed, a frostbitten extremity will be very delicate. Frequently large blisters form, which should be protected. Infection, always a threat, is even more likely if the blisters are broken. Combating infection is hard because the circulation is so poor that antibiotics don't get where they're needed. Don't thaw frostbitten feet if the victim must walk to get out. You'll cause much less damage walking on frozen feet than on thawed feet. The swelling that accompanies thawing will probably mean the victim's boots will no longer fit. The pain may prohibit walking in any case.

Never thaw a part when there is significant danger of it refreezing. Refreezing causes much more damage than allowing a part to remain frozen for a few hours, even a day or so. Also, don't thaw just the frostbitten portion of a hypothermic patient without treating the hypothermia as well. Once the limb is thawed, a good blood supply is crucial. The vasoconstriction caused by the hypothermia will deprive the thawed limb of blood when it needs it most.

Never rub a frostbitten limb with snow. The idea that such cold therapy was helpful came from the observations of Baron Larrey, surgeon-general of Napoleon's army during the retreat from Moscow in the winter of 1812–1813. Frostbite was epidemic. The soldiers thawed their limbs each night over a fire, then refroze them during the day. Infection ran wild, and many soldiers lost fingers, toes, and more. Larrey concluded that heat of any kind caused infection. He was certainly right about the harmful effects of excessive heat, but wrong that the solution was to treat cold injury with cold.

Actual freezing isn't necessary to damage limbs from cold. Trench foot occurs when the victim's feet stay wet and cold continuously for days on end. Common symptoms include swelling, redness, blisters, and nerve damage. The damage can be permanent, and is sometimes so severe, if the exposure to cold continues for weeks, that amputation becomes necessary. Although trench foot is potentially very serious, prevention is simple. Remove your boots every night, dry your feet, warm them if they're cold, and give them a good massage to promote circulation. Treatment in most cases is equally simple: Keep your feet dry, warm, and elevated (to reduce the swelling).

Chilblains can become a minor annoyance to people who expose bare skin to wet, windy conditions with the temperature above freezing. The skin becomes red, rough, dry, and itchy and sometimes cracked. Most people with chilblains would say they have badly chapped skin. Put on a moisturizing lotion, keep the skin warm, and it will soon be fine.

Preventing hypothermia and frostbite takes savvy, conscientious care of your body and adequate gear. Going a little further and becoming truly at ease in winter weather takes a little more of each of those ingredients. I think you'll find that the rewards for the effort are high indeed.

Marilyn, my client on McKinley, did hardly anything right on her way up to 17,200 feet. But she learned, and she had the courage to keep trying even after a serious bout of hypothermia. Five days after reaching 17,200 feet, she stood on the summit, warm, relaxed, and about as happy a person as I've ever seen. For her, learning to deal with the cold made a longstanding dream possible. Climbing McKinley was one of the most satisfying adventures of her life. I hope that learning to live comfortably in the cold will bring as many rewards to you.

APPENDIX:
MY PERSONAL
LAYERING SYSTEM

This is the clothing I bring for a typical winter outing. The amount you will need may vary.

For a one-day ski tour when the temperature is above zero:

- thin long underwear top and bottom
- medium long underwear top and bottom
- fleece sweater with hood
- fleece sweater without hood
- shell jacket and pants
- fleece ski hat
- two pairs of light fleece gloves
- one pair of thick waterproof/breathable gloves with synthetic insulation
- one pair of overmitts with removable fleece liners
- sunglasses
- goggles
- neoprene face mask
- one pair of light liner socks
- one pair of heavy wool socks
- vapor-barrier socks
- double ski-touring boots
- uninsulated gaiters

If I'm going on an overnight ski tour, I bring everything on the list above and add:

- fleece bibs
- down jacket
- a second pair of liner socks
- a second pair of heavy wool socks

If I'm going on a high-altitude expedition, I bring everything on the two lists above except the uninsulated gaiters and add:

- a third pair of long underwear bottoms
- vapor-barrier shirt
- a third fleece jacket
- one pair of heavy mittens
- insulated supergaiters

If you're having trouble locating the gear you need locally, try one of the big outdoor mail-order outfits.

Campmor
P.O. Box 700
Upper Saddle River, NJ 07458–0700
800-226-7667
http://www.campmor.com

Eastern Mountain Sports
1 Vose Farm Road
Peterborough, NH 03458
888-INFO-EMS (888-463-6367)
http://www.emsonline.com

REI
P.O. Box 1938
Sumner, WA 98390
800-426-4840
http://www.rei.com

INDEX